FLASHP●INTS IN
HISTORY

Exploring the causes, effects and triggers of major 20th-century events

Ben Hubbard

An Hachette UK Company
www.hachette.co.uk

This edition published in 2016 by Bounty Books,
a division of Octopus Publishing Group Ltd
Carmelite House
50 Victoria Embankment
London, EC4Y 0DZ
www.octopusbooks.co.uk

First published in 2016 by Bounty Books, a division of Octopus Publishing Group Ltd
Copyright © Octopus Publishing Group Ltd 2016

ISBN: 978-0-75372- 837-6

A CIP catalogue record for this book is available from the British Library

Acknowledgements
Publisher: Samantha Warrington
Design: The Urban Ant Ltd
Art Director: Miranda Snow
Editor: Phoebe Morgan
Picture Research: Nick Wheldon
Senior Production Manager: Peter Hunt

Printed and bound in Hong Kong

10 9 8 7 6 5 4 3 2 1

CONTENTS

1900–1920

The 20th century began with a sense of great optimism. Colonialism and the Industrial Revolution had brought wealth and power to the imperial nations of Europe, as extraordinary breakthroughs in science and invention promised the dawn of an exciting new epoch. The 20th century was an age of tremendous change in the fields of science, politics, economics, exploration, culture and medicine. But nowhere was the progress as rapid than in technology, where greater advances were made in the 20th century than in all of the previous centuries put together. It did not take long for technology from the year 1900 to become outdated, in transportation terms alone. Then, the horse remained the main form of transport for many, while the steam train was still regarded as the latest technological wonder. Within a few years, however, ordinary workers were driving their own motorcars and powered flight had gone from being an aviation fantasy to a commonplace reality. Even sea travel was given a modern makeover: the grand opulence of *Titanic* thrilled and then stunned the world, as man's hubristic belief in his own inventions led to the first great tragedy of the new century. It would not be the last. Great breakthroughs in military technology, combined with shifting ideologies and old rivalries, made the 20th century the most violent in world history. The years from 1900 to 1920 would offset invention, exploration and the struggle for equal rights against revolution and the first worldwide war. This conflict would create unprecedented levels of death and destruction, as the old imperial powers fell and the borders of Europe were redrawn.

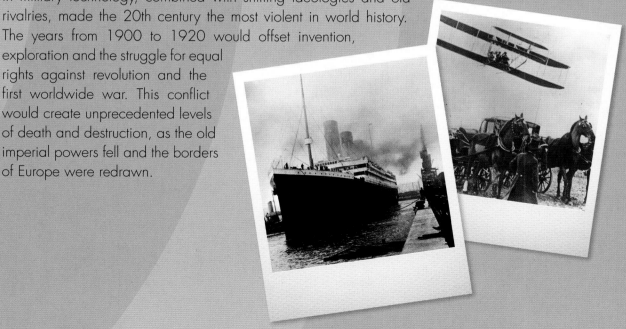

1903

THE WRIGHT BROTHERS' FIRST FLIGHT

'By original scientific research, the Wright brothers discovered the principles of human flight. As inventors, builders and flyers, they further developed the aeroplane, taught man to fly, and opened the era of aviation.'

– A plaque adorning the Wright brothers' *Flyer* at the Smithsonian Institution, USA

17 December 1903 was a good day for flying in the sleepy fishing hamlet of Kitty Hawk, North Carolina. At 10.30am, Orville Wright climbed aboard his *Flyer* biplane as a steady headwind blew across the beach in front of him. Lying flat on the plane's wing section, Orville tested the horizontal lever that controlled lift and descent and then released the restraining wire. History was about to be made. The moment was the culmination of years of research into flight that began when Orville and Wilbur's father bought them a windup 'helicopter' toy powered by a rubber band. As adults the Wright brothers became flying fanatics, experimenting with the rules of aviation in a home-made wind tunnel and testing out their theories during hundreds of glider flights. The brothers concluded an aircraft would have to be powered by an engine to sustain its lift, and set about building one light enough to sit on a glider fuselage. On the morning of 17 December

Orville Wright navigates the skies over Ohio's Huffman Prairie in *Flyer III*, which was first launched in 1905.

1903, the *Flyer* rushed along the remote beach at Kitty Hawk and took to the skies. The first sustained powered flight in history was short: the *Flyer* stayed in the air for 12 seconds and covered a distance of 36m (118ft), but more trials were made that day. During one, Wilbur was able to achieve a successful 59-second flight that covered 259m (850ft). However, the Wright brothers received little recognition for their achievements at the time. Local newspapers reacted with disbelief to their claim, and their secrecy over flying demonstrations led some to label them as 'bluffers'. Despite building new and better *Flyers*, it wasn't until 1908 that the Wright brothers' claims achieved legitimacy. Then, thousands flocked to see a series of demonstrations in France that made the brothers world famous overnight. Today, the Wright brothers are remembered as the flight pioneers who developed the first aeroplane and made it fly.

FLASHPOINT FACT

Neither of the Wright brothers ever married. Orville once said he did not have time for both a wife and an aeroplane.

TIMELINE

1783 The French Montgolfier brothers carry out the first flight of a hot-air balloon over Paris.

1853 George Cayley's *New Flyer* takes his footman across Brompton Dale in the first manned glider flight.

1896 The Wright brothers take an active interest in aviation, developing and building gliders in their bicycle workshop.

1904–5 The Wright brothers develop a practical aeroplane near Dayton, Ohio.

1908 The Wright brothers begin to manufacture aeroplanes.

| 1783 | 1804 | 1853 | 1893 | 1896 | 1900 | 1903 | 1904–5 | 1908 |

1804 English aviation engineer George Cayley develops a model glider with a fixed main wing.

1893 During the first controlled flights in a glider, Otto Lilienthal covers distances of up to 230m (754ft).

1893 The Wright brothers begin to sell and repair bicycles.

1903 The Wright brothers achieve the first sustained powered flight in history.

1900 The Wright brothers begin experimenting with their gliders at Kitty Hawk, North Carolina.

FLASHPOINTS

1896
FLIGHT INVESTIGATIONS BEGIN

The Wright brothers began funding their experimentation into flight by opening a bicycle repair shop in Ohio in 1896. Spurred on by the gliding attempts of Germany's Otto Lilienthal, the brothers decided that pilot control was paramount to successful flying and that this could be achieved by powering a plane with an engine. The brothers also investigated wing shapes and created 'wing warping', a method of twisting a wing to aid lateral control in the air. Wing warping was a precursor to the ailerons used today in modern aviation, which prevent an aircraft from rolling.

1900
TRIALS AT KITTY HAWK

With its soft sand and regular winds, the remote Kitty Hawk became the Wright brothers' regular testing ground for their glider flights. The brothers began trialling manned and unmanned gliders in 1900, using the biplane model favoured in Europe. Despite flying for up to 122m (400ft), the brothers struggled with turning their craft and attaining lift while in flight. To remedy these problems, the brothers conducted more theoretical tests with miniature wings and a specially constructed wind tunnel. As a result, the brothers designed a longer, narrower wing that had an enhanced lift-to-drag ratio and is similar to the modern aircraft wings used today.

An early glider at Kitty Hawk.

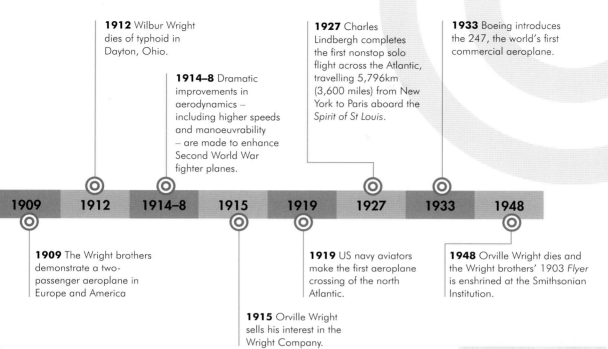

1912 Wilbur Wright dies of typhoid in Dayton, Ohio.

1914–8 Dramatic improvements in aerodynamics – including higher speeds and manoeuvrability – are made to enhance Second World War fighter planes.

1927 Charles Lindbergh completes the first nonstop solo flight across the Atlantic, travelling 5,796km (3,600 miles) from New York to Paris aboard the *Spirit of St Louis*.

1933 Boeing introduces the 247, the world's first commercial aeroplane.

| 1909 | 1912 | 1914–8 | 1915 | 1919 | 1927 | 1933 | 1948 |

1909 The Wright brothers demonstrate a two-passenger aeroplane in Europe and America

1919 US navy aviators make the first aeroplane crossing of the north Atlantic.

1948 Orville Wright dies and the Wright brothers' 1903 *Flyer* is enshrined at the Smithsonian Institution.

1915 Orville Wright sells his interest in the Wright Company.

1905
FLYERS OR LIARS?

Following the success of their first flight in 1903, the Wright brothers went on to achieve a 38-minute flight in 1905 that covered 40km (24.5 miles). The press, however, did not attend the flight and remained unconvinced of the brothers' 'alleged accomplishments'. This scepticism was amplified in Paris, where an article on the brothers was headlined 'FLYERS OR LIARS?' The brothers added to the controversy by refusing to make any further flight demonstrations until they had been offered a contract to produce planes for a commercial company or the military. In 1908, contracts with the US military and a French syndicate rested on the brothers' ability to provide a successful demonstration of their *Flyers*. Orville's series of flying demonstrations in Le Mans, France, and Wilbur's demonstrations in Fort Myer, Virginia, made the brothers instant global celebrities.

1909
LAWSUITS

The Wright brothers' Wright Company became embroiled in a long patent lawsuit in 1909 over the use of ailerons by competing aircraft manufacturers. Despite tarnishing the brothers' public image, the lawsuit did not hinder the success of the Wright Company, which sold planes to the US army and also trained pilots. But the business and legal issues took their toll on Wilbur's health, and he died in 1912. In 1915, Orville sold his interest in the Wright Company and in 1917 the brothers' patent expired, signalling the end of legal issues for the company. Orville went on to work as an aircraft consultant and designed fighter planes during the First World War. He spent the last years of his life defending the Wright brothers' place as inventors of the aeroplane and died in 1948.

A glider becomes airborne with a Wright brother on board.

1908

THE INVENTION OF THE MODEL T FORD

Henry Ford: pioneering inventor and entrepreneur.

'If everyone is moving forward together, then success takes care of itself.'

– Henry Ford explains his theory for a prosperous society

When the first Model T Ford rolled off the assembly line in 1908, Henry Ford fulfilled his promise to 'democratize the automobile'. Up until then, the car was a luxury item built by a team of mechanics that only the rich could afford to buy. But Ford's Model T, popularly known as the 'Tin Lizzie', changed all that. To cut costs, the Model T was constructed along an assembly line instead of in a workshop. This enabled a team of workers to perform a specific task on the machine as it travelled down the assembly line trackway. Assembly line production slashed the price of a Model T from $850 to $300, making it the affordable 'motorcar for the multitudes' that Ford had aspired to produce. The Model T became instantly popular, so much so that the Ford factories could not fulfil the millions of orders that poured in. Between 1909 and 1927, Ford sold 15 million Model Ts and opened factories in England, France and Germany to keep up with demand. In the United States, Model T sales comprised up to 40 per cent of the market share, even despite criticisms that the car itself was 'no beauty'. Produced mainly in black, the Model T had a four-cylinder, water-cooled engine, two forward gears, one reverse gear and a top speed of 72kph (45mph). The Model T and assembly line production transformed economies and societies around the world as automobile industries flourished. Tourism became a major industry and gas stations, highways, motels and camp grounds sprang up everywhere as consumers hit the road. A period of urbanization followed as families moved away from rural areas and into new city suburbs. The Model T was prized for its low cost and durability, but it also profoundly changed the way Americans lived, worked and travelled in the 20th century. It also introduced mass consumerism to modern society.

Henry Ford's Model T introduced America to mass consumerism by offering affordable automobiles to ordinary workers.

FLASHPOINT FACT

The Model T often had to be driven uphill backwards, because reverse was its most powerful gear.

TIMELINE

1879 Henry Ford leaves his family farm to move to Detroit and pursue a career in machinery.

1893 The Duryea brothers build the first American petrol-powered car.

1896 Ford shows his first automobile, the 'Quadricycle', to the world.

1902 Ransom E. Olds begins the mass production of US cars at his Oldsmobile factory.

1903 In a partnership with Detroit coal dealer Alexande Malcomson, Ford forms the Ford Motor Company with $28,000 in cash and $21,00 from private investors.

1879	1886	1893	1896	1897	1901	1902	1903	1908

1886 The first modern automobile, the Benz Patent-Motorwagen, is built by German inventor Carl Benz.

1897 German Rudolf Diesel invents the first car powered by a diesel engine.

1901 Ford enters one of his cars in a race at the Detroit Driving Club, Grosse Pointe, Michigan, and wins. The victory brings him much attention from financial backers.

1908 The Model T Ford, or 'Tin Lizzie' is released.

FLASHPOINTS

1896
CAR-MAKING CAREER
After building the 'Quadricycle' in his shed and basement, Henry Ford drove his first ever automobile through the streets of Detroit in 1896. The Quadricycle attracted enough interest from financial backers to enable Ford to form the Detroit Automobile Company in 1899. The company was dissolved in 1901, however, after Ford refused to deliver automobiles he considered of a low quality. Ford similarly left the Henry Ford Motor Company bearing his name after a dispute in 1902. He went on to form his famous Ford Motor Company in 1903.

The Model T: classic, reliable and cheap.

1903
FORD MOTOR COMPANY
Between 1903 and 1908, the Ford Motor Company manufactured the car models A, B, AC, F, R and S, followed by the highly successful Model N. But none matched the skyrocketing sales of the Model T, buyers of which had to be put on a waiting list so the order schedule could be fulfilled. An automobile affordable to middle-income workers, the Model T brought about rapid change to the American economy and the way people lived and worked. Farms became less isolated, the horse became a redundant form of transport, and cities spread outwards into the suburbs, creating a house-buying boom.

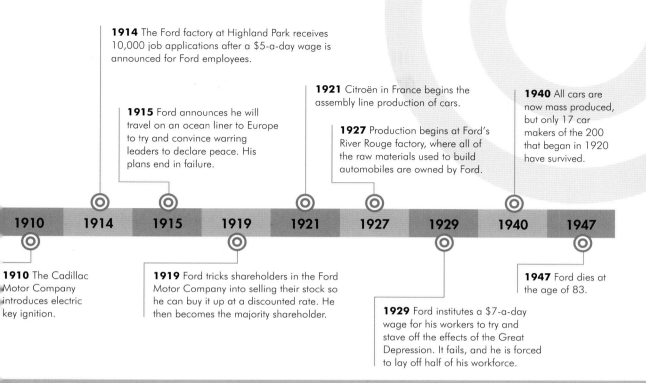

1914 The Ford factory at Highland Park receives 10,000 job applications after a $5-a-day wage is announced for Ford employees.

1915 Ford announces he will travel on an ocean liner to Europe to try and convince warring leaders to declare peace. His plans end in failure.

1921 Citroën in France begins the assembly line production of cars.

1927 Production begins at Ford's River Rouge factory, where all of the raw materials used to build automobiles are owned by Ford.

1940 All cars are now mass produced, but only 17 car makers of the 200 that began in 1920 have survived.

| 1910 | 1914 | 1915 | 1919 | 1921 | 1927 | 1929 | 1940 | 1947 |

1910 The Cadillac Motor Company introduces electric key ignition.

1919 Ford tricks shareholders in the Ford Motor Company into selling their stock so he can buy it up at a discounted rate. He then becomes the majority shareholder.

1929 Ford institutes a $7-a-day wage for his workers to try and stave off the effects of the Great Depression. It fails, and he is forced to lay off half of his workforce.

1947 Ford dies at the age of 83.

1913
ADVANCED PRODUCTION

When Henry Ford's Highland Park factory opened in 1913, it featured the first moving automobile assembly line in the world. This advanced production technology meant a Model T Ford chassis could be turned out every 93 minutes instead of 728 minutes as before. Ford then announced he would pay his employees a $5-a-day wage for an eight-hour work day, rather than the previous $2.34 for a nine-hour day. The improved wage was twice what automobile workers were paid elsewhere and made Ford famous around the world. Branded variously as a humanist and socialist, Ford said he was able to pay his workers more because of the efficiency of production enabled by his assembly line methods. By giving his workers a living wage and offering them reasonably priced goods – such as Model Ts – Ford made his employees consumers. This concept became known as 'Fordism'.

1920
NEWSPAPERS AND PREJUDICE

After purchasing a newspaper called the *Dearborn Independent* in 1919, Ford began publishing anti-Semitic articles under the headline *The International Jew: The World's Problem*. Ford's attacks blamed Jews for provoking violence and financing war. His views won him adulation in Nazi Germany: Adolf Hitler, in particular, was a great admirer of Ford and kept a photo of him in his office. After a libel suit was brought against Ford by Jewish farm co-operative organizer Aaron Sapiro, he was forced to retract his remarks, issue an apology and shut down the newspaper. Ford was later said to have suffered a stroke after seeing newsreel footage taken during the liberation of Nazi concentration camps.

Henry Ford's groundbreaking assembly line.

1911

ROALD AMUNDSEN REACHES THE SOUTH POLE

'The holiday humour that ought to have prevailed in the tent that evening – our first on the plateau – did not make its appearance; there was depression and sadness in the air: we had grown so fond of our dogs.'

– Roald Amundsen describes slaughtering the sled dogs
  for meat during his attempt on the South Pole

By the time Roald Amundsen reached the point where his rival Ernest Shackleton had given up and turned back, victory was close at hand. Aided by fair weather and dog-pulled sleds, Amundsen reached the South Pole on 14 December 1911, and hoisted the Norwegian flag. The explorer, who as a child slept with his window open during winter to prepare for the Arctic cold, made sure each of his four men held the flag as it was planted. The mission had been a team effort, but it was the sled dogs that had seen them over the line. Amundsen knew the value of the dogs, describing them as 'the most important thing for us. The whole outcome of the expedition depends on them.' However, of the 52 dogs that were hand-picked for the mission, only 16 of them saw the South Pole – the rest provided valuable meat for the journey there and back. Amundsen's decision to use dogs was

in grave contrast to the failed Scott expedition that employed ponies and perished to a man after giving chase to the Norwegians. After naming his spot at the South Pole 'Polheim', or 'Pole Home', Amundsen's team turned around and began the long journey home. By the time they reached their expedition base at the Bay of Whales on 25 January 1912, Amundsen's team had travelled for 99 days and covered 2,995km (1,860 miles). Amundsen returned from his adventure a national hero and he continued on other voyages of discovery afterwards. In the end, Amundsen would die in the same heroic manner as he had lived his life: he was killed in 1928 when his plane crashed into the Arctic Ocean during a rescue mission. Amundsen had spoken of his love for the Arctic only a few months earlier, saying, 'If only you knew how splendid it is up there, that's where I want to die.'

Amundsen and his beloved dogs, which towed his sleds across the white Antarctic landscape and won him victory at the South Pole.

FLASHPOINT FACT

Amundsen sent Scott a telegram informing him of his attempt on the South Pole as soon as he departed the Portuguese port of Madeira in 1910.

TIMELINE

1773 Captain James Cook and his crew become the first men to cross the Antarctic Circle.

1823 Englishman James Weddell sails to 74 degrees south – the southernmost point ever sailed. The Weddell Sea today bears his name.

1898 Roald Amundsen and the crew of the *Belgica* become trapped in the pack ice off the Antarctic peninsula and become the first people to survive an Antarctic winter.

1895 Henry Bull lands at Cape Adare and discovers lichen, the first sign of plant life in the Antarctic.

1899 Carsten Borchgrevink and the crew of the *Southern Cross* land at Cape Adare and become the first to spend the winter on Antarctic ground.

1773	1820	1823	1841	1898	1892	1895	1899	1902

1820 Russian Fabian Gottlieb von Bellingshausen becomes the first person to see the Antarctic continent.

1841 While searching for the South Magnetic Pole, James Clark Ross discovers the Ross Sea, Ross Island and the Ross Ice Shelf.

1892 Captain Carl Larsen lands on Seymour Island near the Antarctic peninsula.

1902 Robert Falcon Scott, Edward Wilson and Ernest Shackleton attempt to reach the South Pole, but bad weather forces them to return home.

FLASHPOINTS

1887
STUDIES AT SEA

Although studying to become a doctor on his mother's wishes, the 21-year-old Roald Amundsen quit university for the maritime life as soon as she died. After working on various ships that travelled to the Arctic, Amundsen became first mate on the *Belgica* – the first ship to spend a winter in Antarctica after it became trapped by pack ice in 1887. Amundsen learned valuable lessons from the voyage, including how to prevent scurvy by eating the meat of animals that produce vitamin C.

Roald Amundsen inspects the icy terrain.

1903
NORTHWEST PASSAGE

With a crew of six men aboard his 47-tonne ship the *Gjøa*, Amundsen began a mission to be the first to sail through the Northwest Passage – which connects the Atlantic and Pacific Oceans – and then around the northern Canadian coast. After travelling through the passage and reaching Cape Colborne in 1905, the *Gjøa* was halted by ice and spent the winter on Herschel Island. When the mission was concluded in 1906, Amundsen and his crew were given a heroes' welcome at their final destination of Nome, Alaska. The voyage inspired Amundsen to attempt more 'firsts' and he prepared for a mission to reach the North Pole.

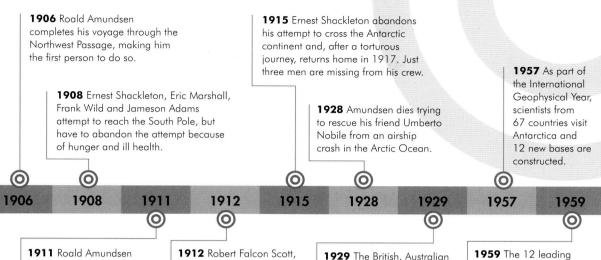

1906 Roald Amundsen completes his voyage through the Northwest Passage, making him the first person to do so.

1908 Ernest Shackleton, Eric Marshall, Frank Wild and Jameson Adams attempt to reach the South Pole, but have to abandon the attempt because of hunger and ill health.

1915 Ernest Shackleton abandons his attempt to cross the Antarctic continent and, after a torturous journey, returns home in 1917. Just three men are missing from his crew.

1928 Amundsen dies trying to rescue his friend Umberto Nobile from an airship crash in the Arctic Ocean.

1957 As part of the International Geophysical Year, scientists from 67 countries visit Antarctica and 12 new bases are constructed.

1906	1908	1911	1912	1915	1928	1929	1957	1959

1911 Roald Amundsen and his team of four men reach the South Pole and return unharmed.

1912 Robert Falcon Scott, Edward Wilson, Edgar Evans and Lawrence Oates reach the South Pole to find Amundsen has beaten them to it. All four die from hunger and cold on the return journey.

1929 The British, Australian and New Zealand Antarctic Research Expedition discovers Mac. Robertson Land and charts much of the nearby Antarctic coastline.

1959 The 12 leading nations that participated in the International Geophysical Year sign the Antarctic Treaty, stating the continent 'shall continue forever to be used exclusively for peaceful purposes'.

1910
ARCTIC OR ANTARCTIC?

Amundsen's plan to sail to the Arctic aboard his new ship the *Fram* changed when he heard that American Robert Peary had reached the North Pole in 1909. Instead, Amundsen prepared the *Fram* to sail to the Antarctic, although he kept the mission a secret from virtually everyone he knew. Amundsen set sail in June 1910 and steered the *Fram* to the Bay of Whales, Antarctica. From the Bay of Whales, Amundsen was 97km (60 miles) closer to the South Pole than his rival Robert Falcon Scott, who also arrived in January 1911 for his attempt on the Pole. In the end, Scott would not reach the Pole until after Amundsen and the mission would then claim his life and those of his men. Amundsen, by contrast, returned home a victorious hero.

1925
ARCTIC FLIGHTS

Following his Antarctic success, Amundsen bought a new ship, the *Maud*, and in 1918 prepared once again to sail to the North Pole. However, he had to abandon his plans and instead set about reaching the North Pole by aeroplane. In 1925, Amundsen and American explorer Lincoln Ellsworth travelled to within 242km (150 miles) of the Pole but did not succeed in passing over it. Then in 1926, Amundsen, Ellsworth and Italian engineer Umberto Nobile managed to fly over the North Pole in an airship. The three men were reported to have thrown their national flags from the airship as they passed over the Pole. Amundsen became embroiled in a dispute over credit for the North Pole flight in his later years, and he died while trying to rescue Nobile from an airship crash near Svalbard in 1928.

The *Fram* in pack ice.

The Norwegian flag flies at the Pole.

1912
THE *TITANIC* SINKS

Captain Edward Smith of the doomed *Titanic*.

'Deeply regret advise you Titanic *sank this morning after collision with iceberg, resulting in serious loss of life. Full particulars later.'*

– White Star Line chairman Bruce Ismay in his telegraph to the White Star Line after surviving the *Titanic* disaster and landing in New York

Titanic begins her maiden voyage from the harbour at Southhampton. It would also be her last.

Titanic was designed to be the last word in ocean travel: a luxurious colossus that could carry 3,547 passengers and was said to be unsinkable. Targeting the large numbers of emigrants and wealthy travellers crossing the Atlantic, *Titanic*'s owners spared no expense fitting out its opulent interior. The ship was described as a floating palace, which featured four elevators, a lavish first-class saloon and a swimming pool. At 269m (882ft) long, *Titanic* was not only the largest but also the most technologically advanced ship in the world. The steamship's double-bottomed hull was divided into 16 compartments, each of which could be closed off if the hull was breached. The ship's architects boasted that even if four of the 16 compartments were flooded, *Titanic* would still stay afloat. Their great error, however, was that the compartments were not capped at the top, leaving a gap for water to move through. In the end, *Titanic*'s maiden voyage was not only destined to be her last: it would also result in the greatest peacetime maritime disaster of the 20th century. The tragedy began around 644km (400 miles) south of Newfoundland, when an iceberg was sighted in *Titanic*'s path. Despite taking evasive action, the ship was travelling too fast to avoid a collision. At 11.40pm the hull on the starboard side of *Titanic* was breached and five of its 16 compartments filled with water. This, in turn, tipped the ship forwards and caused the remaining compartments to also fill with seawater. Two hours and 40 minutes later, *Titanic* sank. With only enough lifeboats for 1,178 of the 2,223 passengers on board, many people perished in the freezing waters. The arrival of the Cunard liner *Carpathia* 80 minutes after the Titanic sank prevented a greater loss of life, but in the end the death toll stood at over 1,500. Intrigue about the passengers' last hours aboard their glamorous and ill-fated vessel continues today in articles, books, television programmes and films.

FLASHPOINT FACT

The wreck of *Titanic* is being slowly consumed by iron-eating micro-organisms.

TIMELINE

1850 The White Star Line is founded.

1907 The idea to build *Titanic* and its Olympic-class sister ships, *Olympic* and *Britannic*, is conceived over dinner between White Star Line chairman J. Bruce Ismay and shipbuilder William James Pirrie.

10 April 1912 At 12 noon, *Titanic* sets sail from Southampton for New York. Four days later she sinks.

May 1912 *Saved from the Titanic*, the first film about the *Titanic* starring actual survivor Dorothy Gibson, is released. Gibson suffers a nervous breakdown after making the film.

May 1912 Insurers Lloyds of London pay the White Star Line £1,000,000 for the disaster. Charities are then set up to provide financial support to those who lost family members, one continuing into the 1960s.

1850	1898	1907	1911	1912	1912	1912	1912	1912

1898 *Futility* is published, a fictional book about a British liner named *Titan* that sinks after hitting an iceberg on her maiden voyage across the Atlantic Ocean, resulting in great loss of life.

1911 *Titanic*'s hull is successfully launched before a crowd of 10,000 spectators.

18 April 1912 The *Carpathia*, carrying *Titanic* survivors, lands in New York to a press frenzy. It takes four days for a full list of the dead to be posted.

April/May 1912 The White Star Line commissions four Canadian ships to recover the bodies of the dead from the sea. Only 333 bodies in total are found.

FLASHPOINTS

1909
GRAND DESIGNS

In 1909 the keel was laid for *Titanic*, one of three Olympic-class ocean liners commissioned by the White Star Line. Designed to outdo their competitor in transatlantic sea travel – Cunard – White Star Line's new ships promised greater levels of speed and luxury to their passengers. The ships would also be the largest sea-going vessels in the world, powered by three main engines and weighing around 46,000 tonnes. Over 600 tonnes of coal a day was needed to power *Titantic*'s engines, enabling a top speed of 45kph (28mph).

1912
DOOMED VOYAGE

Called the 'Millionaire's Special', *Titanic*'s maiden voyage included a range of prominent and wealthy passengers, including American businessman Benjamin Guggenheim, Macy's department-store owner Isidor Straus, White Star Line chairman J. Bruce Ismay and the ship's designer Thomas Andrews. The ship's journey between Southampton and New York was a highly publicized event, proudly celebrated by all involved. However, the hubristic belief that *Titanic* was unsinkable led to basic safety measures being overlooked. These included the low number of lifeboats on board the ship and the reports of icebergs in the area being ignored by some of the ship's crew.

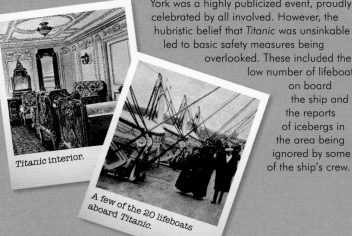

Titanic interior.

A few of the 20 lifeboats aboard Titanic.

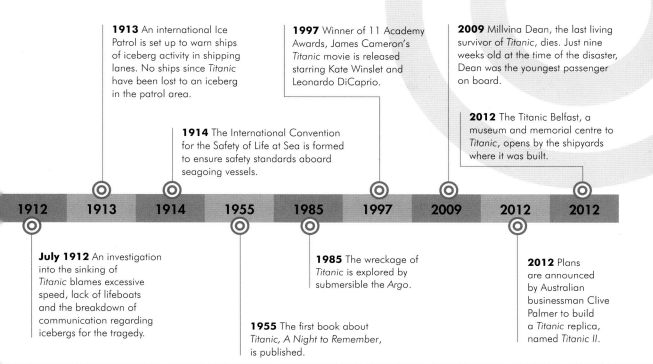

1913 An international Ice Patrol is set up to warn ships of iceberg activity in shipping lanes. No ships since *Titanic* have been lost to an iceberg in the patrol area.

1997 Winner of 11 Academy Awards, James Cameron's *Titanic* movie is released starring Kate Winslet and Leonardo DiCaprio.

2009 Millvina Dean, the last living survivor of *Titanic*, dies. Just nine weeks old at the time of the disaster, Dean was the youngest passenger on board.

1914 The International Convention for the Safety of Life at Sea is formed to ensure safety standards aboard seagoing vessels.

2012 The Titanic Belfast, a museum and memorial centre to *Titanic*, opens by the shipyards where it was built.

1912	1913	1914	1955	1985	1997	2009	2012	2012

July 1912 An investigation into the sinking of *Titanic* blames excessive speed, lack of lifeboats and the breakdown of communication regarding icebergs for the tragedy.

1985 The wreckage of *Titanic* is explored by submersible the *Argo*.

2012 Plans are announced by Australian businessman Clive Palmer to build a *Titanic* replica, named *Titanic II*.

1955 The first book about *Titanic, A Night to Remember*, is published.

1912
TITANIC INQUIRY

A US investigation led by Senator William Alden Smith found contributing factors to *Titanic*'s sinking were the failure of Captain Smith to slow the ship after receiving iceberg warnings and regulatory failures over the lack of lifeboats on board. Passenger testimony also reported that the lifeboats were not launched at full capacity, and that the lack of a general warning meant that many passengers were not aware of the impending danger. The investigation's strongest criticism was meted out to the *Californian*, a ship that was less than 31km (19 miles) away from the sinking *Titanic* and ignored its distress signals. A later British enquiry blamed the excessive speed at which *Titanic* was travelling as the main cause for the collision. The *Titanic* disaster led to changes in maritime safety, and regulations that required all ships have enough lifeboat space for every passenger as well as a compulsory 24-hour radio watch.

1985
THE WRECKAGE REVEALED

Because of the lack of available technology at the time of *Titanic*'s sinking, the first serious attempts to view the wreckage did not come until 1985. Then, a French–American expedition used a 5-m (16-ft) submersible called the *Argo* to take video footage of the wreck and send it to a live monitor above water. Travelling to a depth of 4,000m (13,120ft) at the bottom of the Atlantic Ocean, the *Argo* showed the ship lying upright in two pieces. The footage helped piece together the ship's last moments before it went under and inspired James Cameron's 1997 blockbuster movie, *Titanic*. The movie became the highest-grossing film in history and sparked a renewed round of public interest in the *Titanic* disaster.

An illustration of *Titanic* going down.

1914

ARCHDUKE FERDINAND SHOT

'The lamps are going out all over Europe, we shall not see them lit again in our lifetime.'

– A comment made by British Foreign Secretary Edward Grey in 1914, as Europe stood on the brink of war

Archduke Franz Ferdinand and his wife Sophie were enjoying their wedding anniversary as the couple drove through the streets of Sarajevo on the morning of 28 June 1914. Ferdinand, the heir to the Austro–Hungarian empire, was visiting the Bosnian capital to open a museum and inspect his troops. However, not everyone was pleased about the archduke's visit. Bosnia had been annexed by Austria–Hungary in 1908, and many members of its Serbian population sought independence through revolution. While the archduke and Sophie waved to well-wishers from their open-top car, several Serbian nationalists put their plot to assassinate the archduke into action. As the royal motorcade drove past their supporters, a Serbian assassin threw a bomb at the archduke's car. However, the bomb missed its intended target and instead hit the car following behind. Seeing their plan had been foiled, the rattled conspirators quickly dispersed into the crowd. After taking a break, the archduke insisted on visiting those who had been injured by the bomb and the royal couple once again took to their vehicle. However, their driver had not been informed of the changed itinerary and had to reverse his car into a side road to turn around. By a bizarre twist of fate this happened to be the road where one of the conspirators, Gavrilo Princip, was sitting at a café. As the archduke's driver tried to find the correct gear, Princip crossed the road and fired two shots into the royal car. One of the bullets hit Sophie in her abdomen and the other hit the archduke in the neck. Both were dead by the time their car reached the hospital. The assassination sparked outrage across Europe. Backed up by its ally Germany, Austro–Hungary mobilized its army against Serbia. In response, France and Russia mobilized their forces against Austro–Hungary and Germany. The heavily militarized powers of Europe were now caught up in their own complex network of alliances and counter-alliances. Open war between them broke out in July 1914.

Archduke Franz Ferdinand and his wife Sophie set off on their ill-fated tour of Sarajevo.

FLASHPOINT FACT

The Austro–Hungarian Emperor Franz Josef forbade his son Archduke Franz Ferdinand to attend important state occasions with his wife Sophie, because she was a commoner.

TIMELINE

1882 Germany, Austro–Hungary and Italy form the Triple Alliance.

1906 Britain's launch of the HMS *Dreadnought* brings about a naval arms race with Germany.

1907 France, Britain and Russia form the Triple Entente.

1912 The Balkan War begins as Serbia, Bulgaria and Greece launch an attack against the Ottoman empire. A second war between the Balkan nations in 1913 leaves the region highly unstable.

23 July 1914 Austro–Hungary delivers an ultimatu[m] to Serbia following the assassination of Archduke Ferdinand

1882	1904	1906	1907	1908	1910	1912	1914	1914

1908 Austro–Hungary, backed by Germany, annexes Bosnia–Herzegovina.

28 July 1914 Austro–Hungary declares war on Serbia, signalling the outbreak of the First World War.

1904 Britain and France form an alliance promising mutual support in the event of war.

1910 Germany overtakes Britain as the leading manufacturing nation in Europe.

FLASHPOINTS

1906
EUROPE'S ARM RACE

The beginning of the 20th century saw the great nations of Europe jostling for supremacy by strengthening their militaries. This arms race was intensified in 1906 when Britain launched the HMS *Dreadnought*, the world's first modern battleship. Powered by steam turbines and armed with large deck guns, the *Dreadnought* was the new technological terror of the seas and the great envy of rival Germany. In response, Germany spared no expense in building a modern navy to match Britain's. Russia, France and Austro–Hungary all followed suit, spending heavily on new weaponry and creating massive, conscripted armies.

1907
ALLIES AND ENEMIES

As the imperial powers of Europe competed to have the biggest and best militaries, alliances began to form. Germany, Austro–Hungary and Italy had joined together in the 1882 Triple Alliance, which pitted them against France and Britain in the west and Russia in the east. In response, France, Britain and Russia formed the Triple Entente in 1907. Both alliances obliged their members to support each other if attacked by a hostile power, and they set the stage for the events that followed Archduke Franz Ferdinand's assassination.

HMS *Dreadnought*.

Proud soldiers of the Triple Entente.

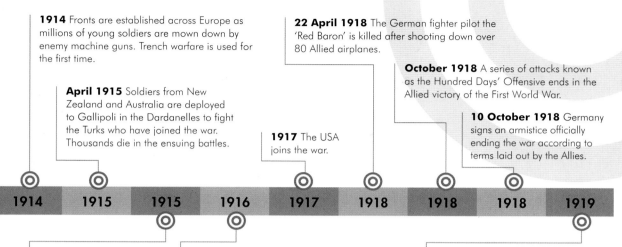

1914 Fronts are established across Europe as millions of young soldiers are mown down by enemy machine guns. Trench warfare is used for the first time.

April 1915 Soldiers from New Zealand and Australia are deployed to Gallipoli in the Dardanelles to fight the Turks who have joined the war. Thousands die in the ensuing battles.

1917 The USA joins the war.

22 April 1918 The German fighter pilot the 'Red Baron' is killed after shooting down over 80 Allied airplanes.

October 1918 A series of attacks known as the Hundred Days' Offensive ends in the Allied victory of the First World War.

10 October 1918 Germany signs an armistice officially ending the war according to terms laid out by the Allies.

1914	1915	1915	1916	1917	1918	1918	1918	1919

April–June 1915 Early bombers and reconnaissance aeroplanes carrying cameras are introduced, as aircraft make their first appearance as weapons of war.

1916 Tens of thousands of allied troops die during assaults on German trenches during the five-month Battle of the Somme.

1916 Nearly 700,000 men lose their lives as the French and British fight the Germans in the Battle of Verdun.

28 May 1919 Germany signs the Treaty of Versailles, which imposes war reparations on the country. The terms of the treaty created resentment among Germans, which added to the rise of Nazi Germany.

1914
ON THE BRINK

Following the assassination of Archduke Franz Ferdinand, Austro–Hungary demanded that Serbia hand his killer over or face military action. Germany backed up this threat, promising to follow Austro–Hungary into war if necessary. Russia, however, vocalized its support of Serbia. France and Britain were obligated by the terms of the Triple Entente to help Russia, while Italy would have to support Germany and Austro–Hungary. Europe was now involved in a crisis that threatened to spark a war between its nations. The people of Europe held their breath.

1914
WAR IS DECLARED

On 28 July 1914, Austro–Hungary carried out its promise against Serbia by bombing Belgrade. This officially began the First World War. Russia quickly mobilized its army in support of Serbia. In August, Germany declared war on Russia and then on France, after the French army mobilized to support Russia. Britain then declared war on Germany. Italy responded to the various declarations of aggression by dropping out of the Triple Alliance altogether. Millions of soldiers across Europe now moved into position ready to fight. Although many hoped the war would be over by Christmas, they would be sadly mistaken. Lasting over four years, the First World War would go on to claim the lives of 16 million people and seriously wound 20 million more.

Representatives thrash out the details of the Treaty of Versailles.

1917
THE OCTOBER REVOLUTION

'Under socialism all will govern in turn and will soon become accustomed to no-one governing.'

– Vladimir Lenin explains his Marxist-led manifesto

A group of young Bolsheviks fly the red flag on a captured armoured car after the success of their October Revolution.

On the morning of 7 November 1917, armed Bolsheviks seized power in the Russian capital of St Petersburg to ignite the country's second revolution of the year. The uprising began when the Bolsheviks occupied the city's public buildings, including its telephone exchange, state bank and railway stations. Next, the Red Guards – a paramilitary group made up of factory workers, peasants and soldiers loyal to the Bolshevik cause – surrounded the Winter Palace, which had the recently elected Cabinet inside. Bolshevik leader Vladimir Lenin commanded a shot be fired from the battleship *Aurora* on the Neva River to signal the start of the insurrection: the October Revolution had begun. A small number of soldiers made up of Cossacks and the Women's Death Battalion tried to defend the Winter Palace, but surrendered after the *Aurora* shelled them into submission. With the palace captured, Cabinet members of the provisional government were rounded up and arrested. The government had been created to bring democracy to Russia after the March Revolution, which had ended with the abdication of Tsar Nicholas II. But there was little consensus about what kind of state should replace the tsardom, and the Bolsheviks took advantage of the confusion to seize control for themselves. Led by Lenin and Leon Trotsky, the Bolshevik party was founded on the principles of Karl Marx, who believed in a communist state where private property was abolished and everybody worked towards the common good. Although the Bolsheviks had the support of the Russian workers' councils – called soviets – and promised 'peace, land and bread' to the common people, Lenin's true intentions soon became clear. He believed that Russia could only become a utopian socialist state through a 'dictatorship of the proletariat'. His pursuit of this utopia led to Russia's civil war and the formation of a repressive Soviet state under Joseph Stalin.

FLASHPOINT FACT

In 1913, Tsar Nicholas II had sole rule over Russia, a giant empire that stretched over 6,440km (4,000 miles) from Europe to Alaska, and contained over 125 million people.

TIMELINE

1894 Tsar Alexander III dies after a sudden illness and his son Nicholas II becomes the ruler of Russia.

1903 The Russian Social Democratic Labour party splits into two rival factions: Mensheviks, or 'minority', and Bolsheviks, 'majority'.

June 1905 Sailors on the battleship *Potemkin* mutiny over their poor-quality rations, adding to the revolutionary spirit gripping Russia.

October 1905 Marxist revolutionary Leon Trotsky returns from exile and helps form an elected council of workers in St Petersburg, called the Petrograd Soviet.

December 1905 Revolutionar[y] groups of Mensheviks and Bolsheviks lead an armed uprisi[ng] in Moscow, occupying public buildings. Moscow is retaken aft[er] heavy government shelling.

September 1906 The Fundamental Laws of 1906 are released, setting out the promises made in the October Manifesto.

| 1894 | 1895 | 1903 | 1905 | 1905 | 1905 | 1905 | 1905 | 1906 | 1906 |

1895 Vladimir Lenin is arrested and kept in solitary confinement for 13 months for producing the Marxist newsletter, *The Workers' Cause*. He is then exiled to Siberia for three years.

January 1905 Soldiers fire on a peaceful march to present a petition to Tsar Nicholas II. The unrest following this 'Bloody Sunday' massacre ignites the first Russian Revolution.

October 1905 The revolution ends after Tsar Nicholas II's October Manifesto promises the formation of an elected parliament, the Duma.

September 1906 Trotsky and other leaders of the Petrograd Soviet are sentenced to imprisonment in Siberia. Trotsky escapes and spends the next decade in exile.

March 1917
TSARDOM ENDS

The March Revolution – the first of two revolutions that made up the Russian Revolution of 1917 – began when workers in St Petersburg went out on strike over food shortages. The imperial army was ordered to arrest the strikers, but many of the soldiers switched sides and joined the workers instead. Tsar Nicholas II refused to order his men to fire on the protesting crowd and the strikers, known as the Petrograd Soviet, became powerful enough to force the tsar to abdicate. In his place, a provisional government was formed to create a democratic style of rule.

September 1917
RED GUARD ARMED

Although the Petrograd Soviet was a rival to the new provisional government and its leader Alexander Kerensky, Kerensky was more concerned about the Russian army. Fearful the army might overthrow the provisional government, Kerensky set about arming the Petrograd Soviet. This new military force became known as the Red Guard. As the Bolsheviks Leon Trotsky and Vladimir Lenin gained a majority in the Petrograd Soviet, the stage became set for their military coup of the provisional government using the Red Guard as muscle.

Tsar Nicholas II after his abdication.

The Red Guard during its conflict with the White Army.

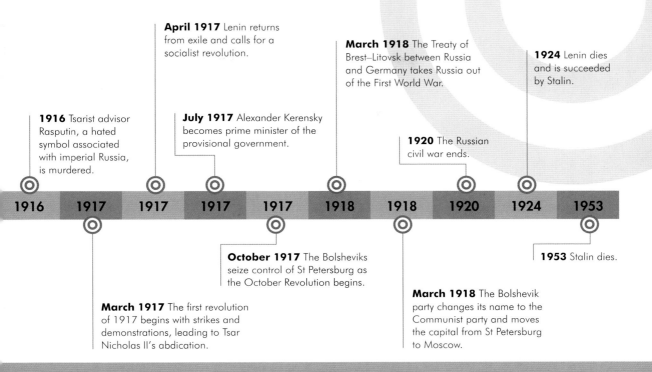

April 1917 Lenin returns from exile and calls for a socialist revolution.

March 1918 The Treaty of Brest–Litovsk between Russia and Germany takes Russia out of the First World War.

1924 Lenin dies and is succeeded by Stalin.

1916 Tsarist advisor Rasputin, a hated symbol associated with imperial Russia, is murdered.

July 1917 Alexander Kerensky becomes prime minister of the provisional government.

1920 The Russian civil war ends.

| 1916 | 1917 | 1917 | 1917 | 1917 | 1918 | 1918 | 1920 | 1924 | 1953 |

October 1917 The Bolsheviks seize control of St Petersburg as the October Revolution begins.

March 1918 The Bolshevik party changes its name to the Communist party and moves the capital from St Petersburg to Moscow.

1953 Stalin dies.

March 1917 The first revolution of 1917 begins with strikes and demonstrations, leading to Tsar Nicholas II's abdication.

January 1918
DEMOCRATIC DREAMS DASHED

After seizing power in St Petersburg, the Bolsheviks set out to consolidate their control of all Russia in December 1917. This started the three-year civil war between the Bolshevik Red Army and the forces that opposed them, known as the White Army. Back in St Petersburg, a Constituent Assembly was elected in January 1918; few of them were Bolsheviks. Determined to maintain complete control, Lenin dissolved the Assembly at gunpoint and in doing so denied Russia its chance to become a democracy. Later that year, the Bolsheviks had Tsar Nicholas II and his family murdered in the cellar of the house where they were imprisoned.

December 1922
SOVIET UNION FORMED

Despite foreign soldiers being sent to help the White Army fight the Red Army, no-one could stop the Bolsheviks prevailing. By the end of 1922 the Bolsheviks, now renamed the Communists, ruled over the whole of Russia. With the red star and hammer and sickle as their insignia, the Communists founded the Union of Soviet Socialist Republics – a single-party state led by Lenin. Despite hopes for a world revolution, Russia was the only country with a Marxist movement that successfully retained power. Joseph Stalin, who replaced Lenin as party leader in 1924, contradicted the notion of a world revolution by saying that socialism was only possible in one country. Stalin's totalitarian rule became the true legacy of the Bolsheviks' October Revolution. Under Stalin, many of the old Bolsheviks were accused of treason and executed, along with millions of other 'enemies of the Soviet people'.

Profile
EMMELINE PANKHURST

Leader of the British suffragette movement, Emmeline Pankhurst.

'Men make the moral code and they expect women to accept it. They have decided that it is entirely right and proper for men to fight for their liberties and their rights, but that it is not right and proper for women to fight for theirs.'

– Emmeline Pankhurst on the importance of the suffragette cause.

Emmeline Pankhurst is escorted from a suffragette movement by police: she was arrested on multiple occasions.

In 1908, Emmeline Pankhurst was imprisoned after trying to invade parliament to present a petition to British prime minister H.H. Asquith. Never one to sit quietly, the suffragette leader railed loudly against her six-week confinement and the rats, the meagre meals and the 'civilized torture of solitary confinement and absolute silence' that she was made to endure. It would not be Pankhurst's only spell inside: she was imprisoned 14 times for her activities in the Women's Social and Political Union (WSPU), an organization she founded in 1903 to win women the vote. Pankhurst advised the members of the WSPU, known as the 'suffragettes', that direct action was needed to bring about a change of government policy. 'Deeds not words, was to be our permanent motto,' Pankhurst later wrote. The WSPU's early activities took non-violent forms that included rallies, speeches and petitions, but its methods changed when a

1905 bill for women's suffrage was rejected in parliament. Standing outside the Houses of Parliament, members of the WSPU began to protest loudly at the news and had to be forcibly removed by police. The publicity caused by the protest gave Pankhurst the idea to adopt a more militant approach. From that point on, the WSPU pursued measures that included violent demonstrations, window smashing, arson and hunger strikes. The behaviour was considered highly unfeminine and unseemly, especially for Pankhurst herself, a mother of five. The police often retaliated aggressively to the WSPU protests, reportedly punching protesters and pulling their breasts during one particularly heated march. The campaign of violence, however, did not last. Pankhurst halted the suffrage activities at the outbreak of the First World War, so that her WSPU members could join the war effort. The contribution of women during the war encouraged several countries to grant them the vote. In Britain this came about in 1928, the year of Pankhurst's death.

FLASHPOINT FACT

Despite taking part in hunger strikes, Emmeline Pankhurst was never force-fed in prison. But Sylvia, her daughter, was force-fed a total of 13 times.

TIMELINE

1867 John Stuart Mill raises the issue of women's suffrage in the British House of Commons.

1893 New Zealand becomes the first nation in the world to give women the vote.

1904 The International Women Suffrage Alliance is founded in Berlin.

1907 A Women's Social and Political Union (WSPU) breakaway group, The Women's Freedom League, is formed.

1913 The WSPU begins its national arson campaign.

1913 The Cat and Mouse Act is passed, permitting the release of hunger-striking suffragettes from prison and their rearrest after they had started eating.

1867	1889	1893	1897	1904	1907	1909	1913	1913	1913

1889 Emmeline and Richard Pankhurst form the Women's Franchise League.

1909 The WSPU introduces violent tactics to further its cause.

1913 US suffragette organization the Feminist Congressional Union begins a campaign of civil disobedience and pickets the White House to publicize its cause.

1897 The National Union of Women's Suffrage Societies (NUWSS) is formed.

FLASHPOINTS

1879
POLITICAL BEGINNINGS

Born to activist parents, Pankhurst became a self-confessed suffragette at the age of 14 but didn't became an activist until after her marriage to Richard Pankhurst in 1897. Richard Pankhurst was a lawyer who had formed the National Society for Women's Suffrage and was the author of the 1882 Married Women's Act, which gave wives control over their money. He supported Emmeline in her suffragette struggle and helped her found the Women's Franchise League, which aimed to win women the right to vote in local elections. Richard's death in 1889 was a great blow to Emmeline and she was forced to bring up their five children alone.

1912
VIOLENCE AND TRAGEDY

On 4 March 1912, Emmeline Pankhurst's WSPU wrought havoc in central London by smashing shop windows in the West End and attacking government buildings. The increasingly militant behaviour of the WSPU reached fever pitch in 1913, when suffragette Emily Davison was killed after throwing herself in front of the king's horse at the Epsom Derby. Jail authorities, who at first had resorted to force-feeding suffragettes on hunger strikes, changed their policy after the Cat and Mouse Act allowed hunger-striking prisoners to be freed and then rearrested after regaining their health.

Emmeline Pankhurst appeals to both men and women during a rally.

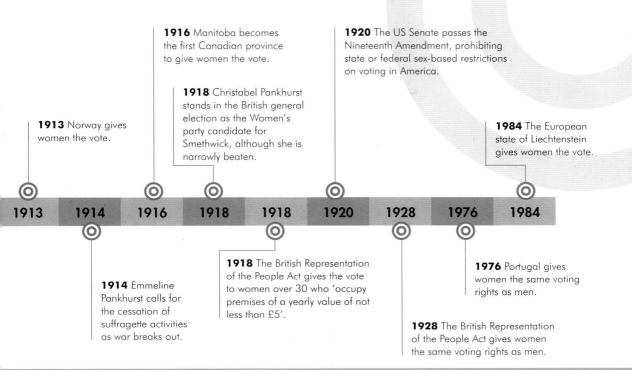

1913 Norway gives women the vote.

1916 Manitoba becomes the first Canadian province to give women the vote.

1918 Christabel Pankhurst stands in the British general election as the Women's party candidate for Smethwick, although she is narrowly beaten.

1920 The US Senate passes the Nineteenth Amendment, prohibiting state or federal sex-based restrictions on voting in America.

1984 The European state of Liechtenstein gives women the vote.

| 1913 | 1914 | 1916 | 1918 | 1918 | 1920 | 1928 | 1976 | 1984 |

1914 Emmeline Pankhurst calls for the cessation of suffragette activities as war breaks out.

1918 The British Representation of the People Act gives the vote to women over 30 who 'occupy premises of a yearly value of not less than £5'.

1928 The British Representation of the People Act gives women the same voting rights as men.

1976 Portugal gives women the same voting rights as men.

1914
WARTIME HIATUS

At the outbreak of the First World War, Emmeline Pankhurst urged women in Britain to give up the suffragette fight so they could help with the war effort. She travelled to the United States, Canada and Russia to encourage the mobilization of women and lived in the United States after the war. After admitting to the valuable contribution made by women during the war, the British government passed the Representation of the People Act 1918, which gave women over the age of 30 the right to vote.

Members of the American suffragette movement.

1928
SUFFRAGETTE SUCCESS

After the war, Pankhurst was still an advocate for women's rights and an ardent suffragette, but she no longer advocated the militant approach. When parliament passed a law allowing women to become ministers of parliament, Pankhurst worked tirelessly on her daughter Christabel's campaign – although in the end she was not elected. In March 1928, the British government introduced the Representation of the People (Equal Franchise) Act to give women the same voting rights as men. The bill became law in July, a few weeks after Emmeline Pankhurst's death.

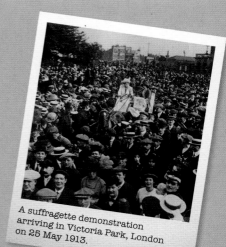

A suffragette demonstration arriving in Victoria Park, London on 25 May 1913.

1920–1940

After the devastation of the First World War, the 1920s introduced a period of prosperity in Europe and the United States. Often known as the 'Jazz Age', it was a time of dramatic social and political change, as an economic boom led to the widespread embrace of mass consumerism. The United States had proven itself to be a global player during the First World War, and now, in the postwar glow, the American public spent freely on home appliances, radios and, before long, a new technology called television. But an unwavering belief in the vibrant US economy led millions of Americans to invest recklessly in the stock market and, in 1929, Wall Street crashed. The Great Depression that followed had dire repercussions for the rest of the world, especially Europe. Here, a continent of contrasts had been created in the aftermath of war. While the victors such as France and Britain enjoyed their postwar prosperity, Germany sagged and seethed under the weight of its war reparations. Europe had a new brand of politics, too, as Russia replaced its Tsarist empire with a Soviet state. But fear over the spread of communism combined catastrophically with the economic downturn, and a menacing new European nationalism emerged. In the mid-1930s, fascist mandates propagated by Benito Mussolini and Adolf Hitler provided an ominous portent of what was to follow. The fragile peace that had lain uneasily over Europe after the First World War was shattered at the end of the decade, as the world was plunged into the most destructive conflict it had ever known.

1926

JOHN LOGIE BAIRD SHOWS TV TO THE WORLD

'The image of the dummy's head formed itself on the screen with what appeared to be almost unbelievable clarity… I ran down the little flight of stairs to Mr Cross's office and seized by the arm his office boy William Taynton, hauled him upstairs and put him in front of the transmitter.'

– John Logie Baird describes the moment he first successfully transmitted moving images

On 26 January 1926, members of the Royal Commission and the press were invited to an upper-floor laboratory in Soho, London. According to an attending *Times* reporter, the men had been invited for a 'demonstration of apparatus invented by Mr J.L. Baird, who claims to have solved the problem of television.' Scottish inventor John Logie Baird called his apparatus the 'televisor', and its invention would launch a revolution in communication and entertainment that is today used by billions of people worldwide. Baird's televisor used mechanical rotating disks to scan images into electronic signals and transmit them to a screen. To demonstrate this process to the Royal Commission, Baird filmed himself playing with two ventriloquist dummy heads that he then produced on a screen in front of his audience. Baird had based his televisor on the work of scientist Paul Nipkow, who created an earlier television system using rotating disks but had failed to create

John Logie Baird demonstrates his 'televisor' apparatus in his Soho laboratory.

a discernible image on screen. By improving on Nipkow's design, Baird was able to stun the world by successfully transmitting moving pictures through the phone line from London to Glasgow in 1927. In 1928 Baird transmitted the first TV pictures from Britain to America via undersea cables, and later that year produced the first colour images, which included strawberries and a man in a red-and-white scarf. But Baird was not the only inventor working on televisions. In 1936, the BBC (British Broadcasting Corporation) began its first television service and tested Baird's system alongside an electronic design created by Marconi Electric and Musical Industries (EMI). In the end, the Marconi–EMI system was found to be more efficient and won out over Baird's televisor. Despite the setback, Baird continued to work on his television inventions and reportedly developed an early 3-D television before his death in 1946.

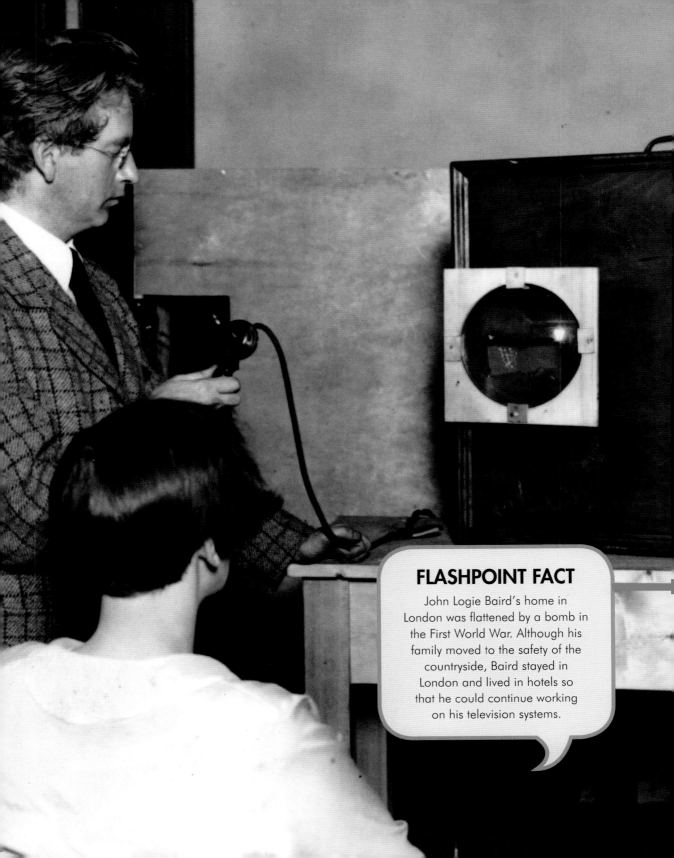

FLASHPOINT FACT

John Logie Baird's home in London was flattened by a bomb in the First World War. Although his family moved to the safety of the countryside, Baird stayed in London and lived in hotels so that he could continue working on his television systems.

TIMELINE

1873 Willoughby Smith discovers selenium, which was used to transform pictures into electrical signals.

1884 German inventor Paul Nipkow patents the Nipkow Disk, a spinning disk that uses a pattern of holes to scan an image.

1900 Constantin Perskyi coins the word 'television' at the International World Fair in Paris.

1928 Television is introduced in the United States.

1922 Vladimir Kosmich Zworykin patents his iconoscope television transmission tube.

1928 American W2XB becomes the first television station in the world.

1873	1880	1884	1897	1900	1922	1925	1928	1928	1928

1880 Alexander Graham Bell and Thomas Edison invent the Photophone, a device they hope will transfer pictures as well as sound.

1925 American inventor Charles Jenkins publicly demonstrates the transmission of moving silhouette images.

1928 The first commercial television set, 'The Daven', is sold for $75.

1897 K.F. Braun invents the cathode-ray tube, which is later used in all modern televisions.

FLASHPOINTS

1923
THE TV SET IS INVENTED

In 1923, the engineer and inventor John Logie Baird built the world's first-ever television set from a hatbox, a pair of scissors, a tea chest, some bicycle lights and the motor from an electric fan in his workshop. He used his TV set to transmit moving silhouette images, but burnt his hand badly when his equipment gave him a 1,000-volt electric shock. Baird was subsequently invited to vacate his Hastings workshop following the incident and relocated to a new laboratory in Soho, London.

1925
AN EARLY TV STAR

From his Soho laboratory, Baird successfully transmitted moving images: first of a ventriloquist dummy and then a 20-year-old office worker called William Edward Taynton. Excited by the breakthrough, Baird visited the offices of *The Daily Express* newspaper to publicize his new invention. In response, the disbelieving news editor of the paper ordered a reporter to escort Baird from the building, saying, 'For God's sake, go down to reception and get rid of a lunatic who's down there. He says he's got a machine for seeing by wireless! Watch him – he may have a razor on him.'

Early commercial TV set.

The rotating disk system used in Logie Baird's televisor.

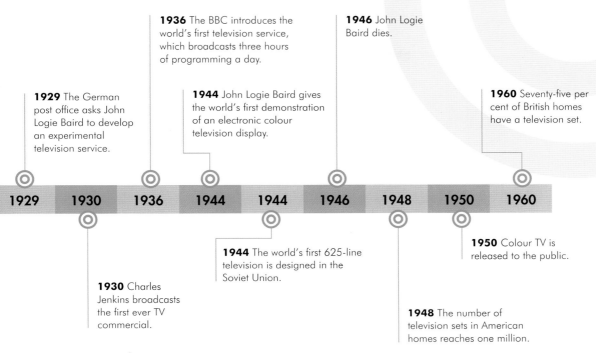

1929 The German post office asks John Logie Baird to develop an experimental television service.

1936 The BBC introduces the world's first television service, which broadcasts three hours of programming a day.

1944 John Logie Baird gives the world's first demonstration of an electronic colour television display.

1946 John Logie Baird dies.

1960 Seventy-five per cent of British homes have a television set.

| 1929 | 1930 | 1936 | 1944 | 1944 | 1946 | 1948 | 1950 | 1960 |

1930 Charles Jenkins broadcasts the first ever TV commercial.

1944 The world's first 625-line television is designed in the Soviet Union.

1948 The number of television sets in American homes reaches one million.

1950 Colour TV is released to the public.

Around 1,000 televisors were made, costing £26 each.

1928
FURTHER FIRSTS

In 1928 John Logie Baird founded the Baird Television Development Company Ltd, which wowed people in Britain and the United States by making the first transatlantic television transmission from London to New York. Baird then made the first-ever television programme for the BBC. Next, Baird devised a way of capturing live events, and televised the Epsom Derby in 1931. He later constructed a theatre-projection system to televise a boxing match on a giant 4.6 by 3.7-m (15 by 12-ft) screen.

1929
FIRES AND THE BBC

In 1929, the BBC used Baird's television system to broadcast its programmes, but from 1936 began alternating between Baird's transmission system and Marconi–EMI's system. The BBC then decided to test both systems alongside each other in a six-month trial. But disaster struck in 1937, when much of Baird's equipment was destroyed in a fire at his London laboratory. The BBC then decided that the Baird system was inadequate because of the lack of mobility posed by its large cameras, hoses, developing tanks and cables. Baird's television systems were then replaced by the electronic television system developed by Marconi–EMI. As the BBC began a regular TV service, the television age began – but it would take place without Baird.

1929
THE WALL STREET STOCK-MARKET CRASH

'So, first of all, let me assert my firm belief that the only thing we have to fear is fear itself.'

– President Franklin D. Roosevelt tries to console the American public during his inauguration speech

The 1920s was boom time in America. As the economy went from strength to strength, millions of Americans invested in the stock market. Even those of meagre means tried to get rich quick by playing the stock market on margin. This meant borrowing money to pay for shares and then using them as collateral against the loan. But at the end of the decade the good times came to a sudden, shuddering halt, as boom turned to bust. On 4 October 1929, the market took a sharp dip and continued to slide throughout the month. 21 October saw an avalanche of selling, as many Americans tried to salvage something from their weakened portfolios. On 24 October – 'Black Thursday' – panic swept the Wall Street stock exchange and investors ordered brokers to sell at any price. Worse was to come on 29 October, known to history as 'Black Tuesday' – the day Wall Street crashed. As the trading day ended, vast fortunes were lost and millions of ordinary Americans found themselves instantly bankrupt.

The stock-market crash then turned into the Great Depression, as millions of Americans lost their jobs, hundreds of banks closed and former millionaires took to selling apples on street corners. Mass misery ensued: some figures reported that over 23,000 people committed suicide in 1929 alone. President Herbert Hoover, however, refused to accept that the Great Depression would last. He proposed tax cuts and asked businesses to slash worker wages. Mass layoffs and unemployment followed: by 1933, 25 per cent of American workers were without work. Hoover's response to the rising unemployment was to encourage private charities to offer help on the ground, as millions of people lost their homes and were forced to join soup kitchens. Hoover's failure to save America's economy led to the election of Democrat Franklin D. Roosevelt, who launched the 'New Deal' and turned America into a social welfare state. Many nations around the world followed Roosevelt's example.

A crowd congregates in New York's Wall Street following news of the stock market crash.

TIMELINE

October 1929 After six years of prosperity, the Wall Street stock market crashes on 29 October. As stock prices plummet, banks call in all loans, which leads to the Great Depression.

March–November 1930 Over 1.6 million people have become unemployed since the crash and the streets of New York city are crowded with thousands of the unemployed selling apples for five cents apiece.

1931 Great Britain, Japan and the countries of Scandinavia leave the gold standard, the monetary system whereby a country's currency has a value linked to gold. There are banking crises in Austria and Germany.

1931 New York's Bank of the United States collapses.

July 1932 The US Reconstruction Finance Corporation is ordered to give money to struggling American states.

1929	1930	1930	1930	1931	1931	1931	1932	1932

1930 The knock-on effect of the Wall Street crash leads to a sharp decline in international trade, contributing to the worst global depression of the 20th century.

February 1931 Food riots break out across the United States and looters make smash-and-grab attacks on grocery stores.

1930 A severe drought starts in the Great Plains area, ruining millions of farms and leading to the Dust Bowl.

1932 Workers in London and other major cities protest over jobs cuts and worsening employment conditions. With public dissatisfaction at an all-time high, extremist groups such as the Nazi party begin to gain support.

FLASHPOINTS

1929
THE CRASH

After the panic selling on Black Thursday, Wall Street financiers tried to stabilize the market by buying up as many shares as they could. This offered a temporary lull, but by Black Tuesday an even greater sense of panic swept the stock-exchange floor. One eyewitness account reported that brokers 'hollered and screamed, they clawed at one another's collars. It was like a bunch of crazy men.' Others collapsed where they stood as the value of shares fell through the floor and selling orders made it impossible for the Exchange to keep up with the transactions. By the end of the day more than 30 billion dollars had been lost — more than twice the national debt.

1930
THE MISERY OF MILLIONS

Following the calamitous events of the 1929 stock-market crash, the Great Depression began. The effects were felt across the world but nowhere as keenly as in North America, where millions lost their jobs, savings and then homes, as they became unable to pay their mortgages. By 1932, the number of homeless people reached more than two million and many were forced to live in large cardboard shantytowns, mockingly called 'Hoovervilles' after the much-maligned president. The food served on the many soup lines was similarly referred to as 'Hoover Stew'.

The Wall Street trading floor in October 1929.

People line up for their Hoover Stew during the Great Depression.

August 1933 The government establishes the Soil Erosion Service in an attempt to address the years of drought blighting the farms of the Great Plains.

October 1936 *The San Francisco News* publishes a series of John Steinbeck articles about the Dust Bowl migrant camps. The articles will later inform his novel, *The Grapes of Wrath*.

March 1933 Franklin D. Roosevelt delivers the first of his radio 'fireside chats', during which he appeals to the nation to join him in 'banishing fear'.

May 1934 A three-day dust storm blows topsoil as far east as New York and Boston, where street lights are lit during the day to enable people to see.

November 1940 Franklin D. Roosevelt is elected to an unprecedented third term as president.

1932	1933	1933	1933	1934	1935	1936	1940	1941

April 1933 President Roosevelt takes the nation off the gold standard under the Emergency Banking Act.

April 1935 Franklin D. Roosevelt creates the Works Progress Administration, which employs over 8.5 million people to build roads, bridges and airports.

1941 The entry of America into the Second World War after the Japanese bombing of Pearl Harbor greatly improves the US economy, as industries create jobs to support the war effort.

November 1932 Franklin D. Roosevelt is elected president in a landslide victory after receiving 22.8 million votes to Herbert Hoover's 15.75 million.

1932
THE NEW DEAL

Despite introducing measures such as the Hoover Dam project to stimulate the economy, President Hoover was heavily defeated by his opponent Franklin D. Roosevelt in the general election of 1932. Roosevelt swept into power on the basis of his 'New Deal' manifesto, which promised change according to the 'Three Rs': Relief, Recovery, and Reform. Under the New Deal, Roosevelt spent over $6 billion on public works to create jobs and revive the economy. He also tried to endear the American public to politicians once more through his evening 'fireside chats' on the radio.

Unemployment marches in the 1930s.

1934
THE DUST BOWL

From 1934 to 1940 a severe drought hit many of the states of the American Great Plains, destroying crops and bringing devastation to entire farming communities. Without plants to anchor the topsoil, wind storms buried a vast region in earth and dust, which then became known as the 'Dust Bowl'. Thousands of families from Kansas, Oklahoma, Texas, New Mexico and Colorado were forced to pack up their homes and travel to California to find seasonal work as a result of the Dust Bowl.

Profile
GANDHI

*'I object to violence because when it appears
to do good, the good is only temporary;
the evil it does is permanent.'*

– Mohandas 'Mahatma' Gandhi explains his advocacy of non-violence

The Second World War marked the turning point in Mohandas 'Mahatma' Gandhi's campaign to end British rule in India. The leader of the Indian National Congress and advocate of non-violent resistance, Gandhi could not tolerate a war that would conscript thousands of Indians into the British army. After launching a programme of civil disobedience in 1930, Gandhi now endorsed a new 'Quit India' campaign, which put the country on the road to freedom. Gandhi had begun his struggle for Indian independence after fighting against racial prejudice as a lawyer in South Africa. On his return in 1915 he called on his countrymen to seek independence from Britain through non-violent means. Gandhi put his methods into action after Britain broke its promise to free India after the First World War. Gandhi's early acts of passive resistance included the boycott of foreign textiles, but after the Amritsar massacre of 1919 he launched the new 'Non-Co-operation Movement'. Gandhi's arrest for his salt marches in 1930 sparked large protests, and tens of thousands were arrested after marching in the streets. Gandhi's 1930 imprisonment was only one of many. His last jail term came in 1942, when Gandhi and his fellow leaders were arrested just hours after launching their Quit India campaign and imprisoned without trial for two years. The Quit India campaign went ahead, but without Gandhi's guidance many of his followers resorted to violent methods, including the sabotage of railway and telegraph lines and the use of bombs. Realizing their days of rule in India were over, the British granted India independence in 1947. However, this resulted in the partition of India to form Pakistan, which led to violence and genocide and left India splintered and brutalized. Gandhi was assassinated by a Hindu extremist in 1948. Today, Gandhi is considered the father of India and his name is forever linked with the civil-rights movement and the fight against oppression.

As with all of his non-violent protests, Gandhi led by example. Here, he spins yarn following his calls to boycott foreign cloth.

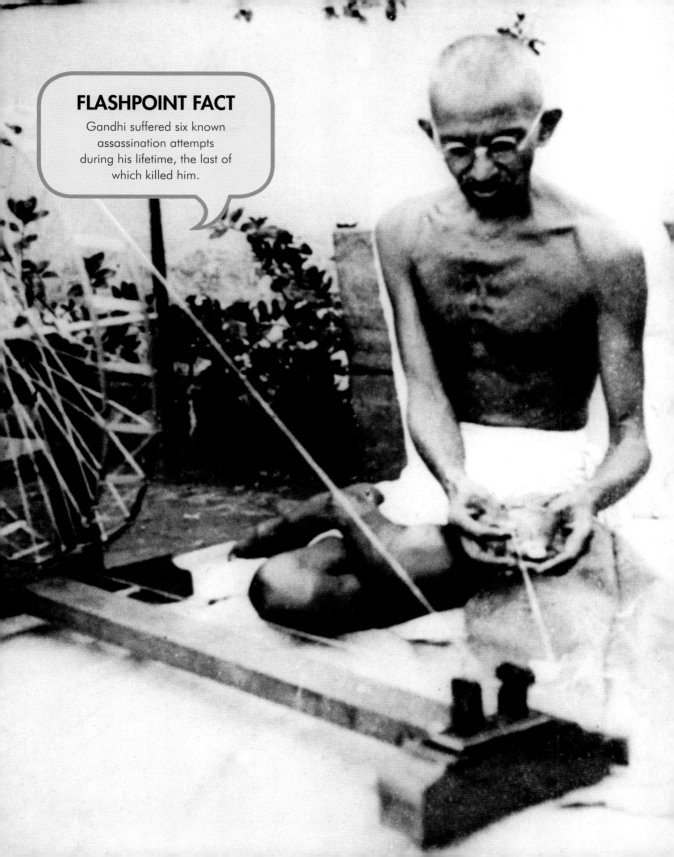

FLASHPOINT FACT
Gandhi suffered six known assassination attempts during his lifetime, the last of which killed him.

TIMELINE

1919 British soldiers kill 379 protesters during the Amritsar massacre in the Punjab region.

1915 Gandhi returns to India after spending 21 years as a barrister in South Africa.

May 1930 Following Gandhi's imprisonment, tens of thousands of his followers are arrested and incarcerated.

1931 After the failed Round Table Conference talks in London, Gandhi visits Lancashire mill workers, who have been affected by the Indian boycott of foreign cloth.

1934 Gandhi becomes a champion of the Untouchables, the lowest caste in Indian society.

| 1915 | 1917 | 1919 | 1922 | 1930 | 1930 | 1931 | 1934 | 1934 | 1935 |

1917 Gandhi launches the non-co-operation campaign of *satyagraha*, formed from the Sanskrit words for 'truth' and 'firmness'.

1922 Gandhi calls for a boycott on imported textiles, which were damaging India's own textile industries. Gandhi encourages Indians to wear home-woven cloth, and dresses himself in simple white clothes, sandals and spectacles.

1930 Women across India follow Gandhi's salt march protest by illegally boiling sea water to make salt.

1935 The Government of India Act grants Indian provinces power over local administrative affairs.

1934 Gandhi launches the All-India Village Industries Association.

FLASHPOINTS

1930 SALT MARCH

After the British government failed to address calls to give India dominion status, Gandhi struck out on his first salt march in 1930. Under British law, it was illegal for Indians to collect or refine salt. In defiance of this law Gandhi walked 386km (240 miles) to the sea, where he gathered a handful of salt. Huge crowds came to support Gandhi in this non-violent action and the rattled British government imprisoned over 60,000 people in response.

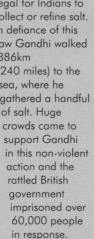

Gandhi leads one of his salt marches.

1931 TALKS IN LONDON

Gandhi's salt march encouraged many others to follow his example and disobey the law on salt, which led to Gandhi's arrest and imprisonment for a second salt march in 1930. As a result of the unrest, Gandhi was invited to London in 1931 to discuss Indian self-rule with British ministers. Known as the Round Table Conference, the talks failed after agreement could not be reached between the British government and the attending Hindu and Muslim representatives. A disappointed Gandhi retuned to India to continue the fight for independence.

Gandhi outside 10 Downing Street, London.

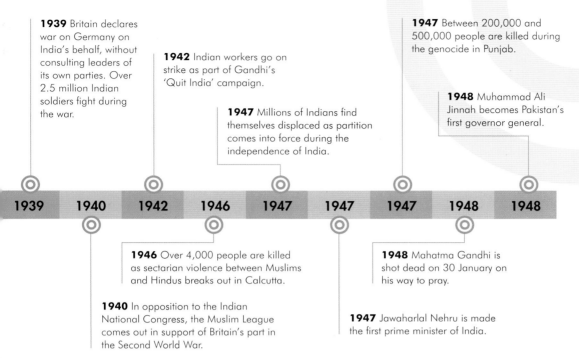

1939 Britain declares war on Germany on India's behalf, without consulting leaders of its own parties. Over 2.5 million Indian soldiers fight during the war.

1942 Indian workers go on strike as part of Gandhi's 'Quit India' campaign.

1947 Millions of Indians find themselves displaced as partition comes into force during the independence of India.

1947 Between 200,000 and 500,000 people are killed during the genocide in Punjab.

1948 Muhammad Ali Jinnah becomes Pakistan's first governor general.

1939	1940	1942	1946	1947	1947	1947	1948	1948

1946 Over 4,000 people are killed as sectarian violence between Muslims and Hindus breaks out in Calcutta.

1948 Mahatma Gandhi is shot dead on 30 January on his way to pray.

1940 In opposition to the Indian National Congress, the Muslim League comes out in support of Britain's part in the Second World War.

1947 Jawaharlal Nehru is made the first prime minister of India.

1942
QUIT INDIA

The Quit India campaign, launched by Gandhi and Indian National Congress leader Jawaharlal Nehru in 1942, was designed to disrupt the British war effort through Indian civil disobedience. It called for the immediate withdrawal of Britain from India. The campaign garnered great support among Indians, who staged strikes and carried out acts of sporadic violence across the country. The British government reacted by arresting nearly the whole of the Indian National Congress leadership and keeping them imprisoned until 1945. Without clear leadership, the Quit India campaign was quickly crushed by the British army. However, the campaign showed Britain that its ongoing governance of India was untenable.

1947
INDEPENDENCE

In 1946, sectarian violence erupted after India's Muslim League party demanded a separate homeland for Muslims as part of a deal for Indian independence. This led to Indian Viceroy Lord Louis Mountbatten's 1947 announcement that India would be partitioned into separate states for Hindus and Muslims. The result was the displacement of millions of Muslims and Hindus on the day of independence, as the separate nations of India and Pakistan were formed. The region of Punjab was split between these two countries, resulting in religious rioting and genocide, and the deaths of hundreds of thousands of people.

Independence day: 15 August 1947.

1933

HITLER BECOMES CHANCELLOR

'The very first essential for success is a perpetually constant and regular employment of violence.'

– Hitler explains his approach to leading a nation

It was in jail that Hitler wrote *Mein Kampf* ('My Struggle'), a memoir outlining his hatred of Jews and his plans for a new world order. When he was released in 1924, the leader of the National Socialist German Workers' party, known as the Nazis, set about putting his plans into action. The effects of the American Great Depression had brought widespread unemployment to Germany, and in 1930 President Paul von Hindenburg exacerbated the situation by slashing government expenditure, worker wages and unemployment benefits. The resulting anger and disillusionment polarized German politics between the extreme left, represented by the communists, and extreme right, represented by the Nazis. Terrified of what the rise of communism could mean for their businesses, wealthy industrialists provided the Nazi party with money and support. Hitler's strong oratory combined with Joseph Goebbels' propaganda campaign effectively targeted many groups within Germany and helped the Nazis' meteoric rise to power. The Nazis promised to return the nation to its place as a militarily strong power and overturn the Treaty of Versailles, which had burdened Germany with a massive debt in war reparations from World War One. Their party manifesto held enough popular appeal to win the Nazis 230 votes in the Reichstag by 1932, which was a monumental increase from the 12 seats the party held in 1928. Despite being the largest party in Germany, Hitler had been narrowly defeated by Hindenburg in the 1932 presidential election, and the Nazi party did not have enough seats to hold a parliamentary majority. However, the minority parties were unable to work together to form a majority government and keep Hitler from power. In 1933, former chancellor Franz von Papen convinced President Hindenburg to elect Hitler as a puppet chancellor, so that they could then control him from behind the scenes. Hitler, however, had no intention of sharing power, and when he was made chancellor on 30 January 1933, the Third Reich was born.

Adolf Hitler addresses a Nazi Party meeting in Munich in 1925. To Hitler's far left is Heinrich Himmler, the architect of the Holocaust.

FLASHPOINT FACT

As a young man, Hitler painted watercolours and wanted to be an artist, but was rejected by Vienna's Academy of Fine Arts. In 2014, one of his paintings was sold at auction for £103,000.

TIMELINE

1918 Hitler is awarded the Iron Cross, First Class, for bravery in action.

1920 The German Workers' party changes its name to the National Socialist German Workers' party, or the Nazi party for short.

1921 The paramilitary Stormtroopers are formed.

1923 Hitler is imprisoned after his beer-hall *Putsch* (coup), but experiences a comfortable incarceration in Landsberg prison.

1925 Hitler's memoir *Mein Kampf* is published.

April 1925 The SS (*Schutzstaffel*, or 'defence squadron') is formed as Hitler's personal bodyguard, later to become the Nazi party militia.

1929 The membership of the Nazi party rises to 180,000 members, from only 25,000 in 1925.

March 1932 Hitler's Stormtroopers engage in street battles with communists and other opponents.

March 1932 Paul von Hindenburg narrowly defeats Hitler in the German presidential election.

| 1918 | 1920 | 1921 | 1923 | 1925 | 1925 | 1929 | 1932 | 1932 |

FLASHPOINTS

1923
BEER-HALL *PUTSCH*

After serving in the German army in the First World War, Hitler moved to Munich and became leader of the National Socialist German Workers' party. In 1923, Hitler attempted to lead his Nazi party into a military coup, or *putsch*, by storming a political meeting in a Bavarian beer hall and announcing that the revolution had arrived. The coup was easily put down by authorities and Hitler was jailed for five years for treason. He was released in 1924 after serving nine months.

1927
THE NUREMBERG RALLY

The first of the notorious Nazi Nuremberg Rallies took place in 1927 before a small crowd. Although the Nazis only controlled three per cent of the vote in 1927, by 1929 their Nuremberg Rallies had grown into the large-scale events that they are remembered as today. Using the medieval city of Nuremberg as the backdrop for the rallies' pomp and pageantry, each one would include large banners, human swastika formations, goose-step marches and Wagnerian overtures played at full volume.

Hitler and various Nazi-party leaders would address the ever-growing rally crowds with rousing oratories that set out Nazi policies and incited racial hatred among the spectators. The 11th rally, entitled the 'Rally of Peace', was cancelled in 1939 so that Hitler could concentrate on invading Poland.

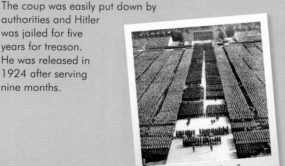
A Nuremberg Rally of the 1930s.

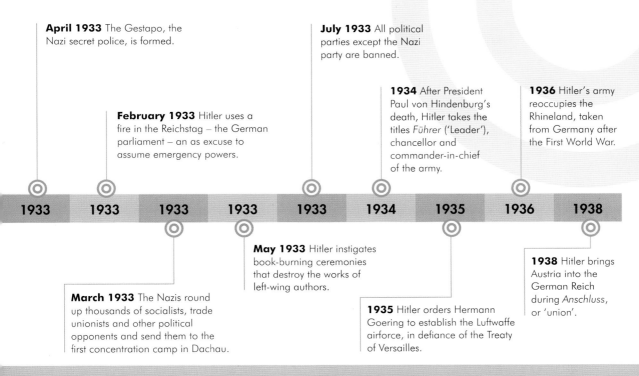

April 1933 The Gestapo, the Nazi secret police, is formed.

July 1933 All political parties except the Nazi party are banned.

1934 After President Paul von Hindenburg's death, Hitler takes the titles *Führer* ('Leader'), chancellor and commander-in-chief of the army.

1936 Hitler's army reoccupies the Rhineland, taken from Germany after the First World War.

February 1933 Hitler uses a fire in the Reichstag – the German parliament – an as excuse to assume emergency powers.

| 1933 | 1933 | 1933 | 1933 | 1933 | 1934 | 1935 | 1936 | 1938 |

May 1933 Hitler instigates book-burning ceremonies that destroy the works of left-wing authors.

1938 Hitler brings Austria into the German Reich during *Anschluss*, or 'union'.

March 1933 The Nazis round up thousands of socialists, trade unionists and other political opponents and send them to the first concentration camp in Dachau.

1935 Hitler orders Hermann Goering to establish the Luftwaffe airforce, in defiance of the Treaty of Versailles.

1934
THE NIGHT OF THE LONG KNIVES

As part of the removal of all limits to his acquisition of power, Hitler forced all other political parties in Germany to disband in 1934 and then set about establishing complete control of the army. To do this Hitler had to silence calls for increased power from within his own paramilitary group, the Stormtroopers, or 'SA', as they were known. He did so by murdering the whole of the SA leadership and all other political opponents in one swoop, in what became known as the 'Night of the Long Knives'. There was no question of the army's support for Hitler after President Hindenburg died in 1934, and the Nazi leader proclaimed himself *Führer* of the country. The officers of the German army swore their unconditional loyalty to Hitler soon afterwards.

1938
KRISTALLNACHT

On the evening of 9 November 1938, Hitler ordered a series of orchestrated anti-Jewish attacks, called *Kristallnacht*, or the 'Night of Broken Glass'. Over the next 48 hours, rioters smashed the storefronts of Jewish businesses, damaged over 1,000 synagogues and attacked any Jews that they saw. German police were complicit in the violence, as the Nazis arrested over 30,000 Jewish men between the ages of 16 and 60 and transported them to concentration camps. *Kristallnacht* was closely followed by the economic and political persecution of the Jews and was the precursor for the Holocaust and Hitler's 'Final Solution', which laid out the blueprint for the mass extermination of Jews in Europe.

The damage from *Kristallnacht*, the 'Night of Broken Glass'.

1936

THE SPANISH CIVIL WAR BEGINS

'We do not believe in government through the voting booth. The Spanish national will was never freely expressed through the ballot box. Spain has no foolish dreams.'

– Francisco Franco issues a statement in 1938 during the Spanish Civil War

It was during his exile in the Canary Islands that General Francisco Franco called for Spanish forces to rise up in a military coup. Heeding Franco's order, right-wing military officers in Spanish Morocco mobilized their forces on 18 July 1936, against the left-wing Republican government of Spain. The Spanish civil war had begun. Within three days, Franco's rebels had captured Morocco and parts of Spain. Cities such as Cadiz, Saragossa and Seville declared their support for Franco's Nationalists, while Barcelona, Madrid and Valencia declared their allegiance to the Republic. Franco's planned overthrow of the government was the result of Spain's deep political divisions that had split the country between the right-wing Nationalists and the left-wing Republicans. The Nationalist party was made up of the Catholic Church, monarchists, landowners and employers; the Republicans were made up of workers, trade unionists, socialists and peasants. This political polarization had come about after the economic knock-on effects of America's Great Depression had led to the collapse of Spain's military dictatorship in 1929 and the abdication of King Alfonso XIII. The country had voted overwhelmingly for the abolition of the monarchy in favour of a liberal government, and in 1932 the Second Republic was formed. However, members of the Spanish military, aristocracy and church opposed the left-wing Republic, and in the 1933 elections right-wing elements regained control of the government. In response, Spanish socialists and anarchists launched failed revolts in 1934, which were put down by General Franco on behalf of the conservative government. In February 1936, a new election put leftist coalition the Popular Front in power, and Franco was exiled to the Canary Islands. By the end of 1936, Franco's rebel army had made significant advances into Spain and he was named head of state of an alternative government. After three years of brutal fighting, Franco would become the victor of the Spanish Civil War and the country's leader until his death in 1975.

A leftist exodus from Malaga begins after the Nationalist army's victory over the city. Franco's airforce and navy bombed the unarmed procession at will.

FLASHPOINT FACT

Between 100,000 and 200,000 people were executed by the Nationalists in their attempts to eradicate 'leftism' from Spain.

TIMELINE

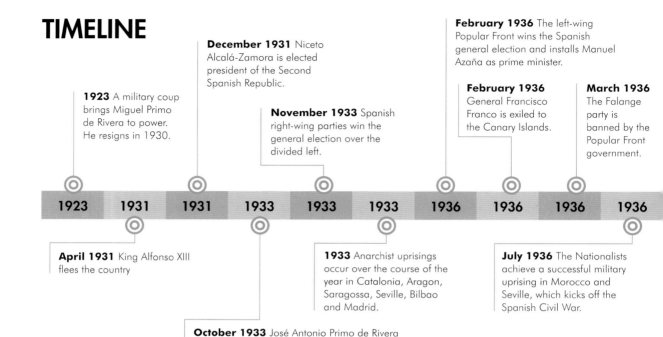

1923 A military coup brings Miguel Primo de Rivera to power. He resigns in 1930.

December 1931 Niceto Alcalá-Zamora is elected president of the Second Spanish Republic.

November 1933 Spanish right-wing parties win the general election over the divided left.

February 1936 The left-wing Popular Front wins the Spanish general election and installs Manuel Azaña as prime minister.

February 1936 General Francisco Franco is exiled to the Canary Islands.

March 1936 The Falange party is banned by the Popular Front government.

| 1923 | 1931 | 1931 | 1933 | 1933 | 1933 | 1936 | 1936 | 1936 | 1936 |

April 1931 King Alfonso XIII flees the country

1933 Anarchist uprisings occur over the course of the year in Catalonia, Aragon, Saragossa, Seville, Bilbao and Madrid.

July 1936 The Nationalists achieve a successful military uprising in Morocco and Seville, which kicks off the Spanish Civil War.

October 1933 José Antonio Primo de Rivera founds the fascist Falange party.

FLASHPOINTS

1933
RISE OF THE RIGHT

In response to concerns over the rising power of Spain's left amidst the economic turmoil brought on by the Great Depression, right-wing groups began to gain support in the early 1930s. These groups included the conservative religious group the Carlists – which was seen as an alternative to the sometimes anti-Catholic doctrines of the left – and the fascist Falange party. Formed by aristocratic lawyer José Antonio Primo de Rivera, the Falangists based themselves on the Italian fascists led by Benito Mussolini and added to the rise of 1930s European fascism, which included Hitler's Nazi party. José Antonio Primo de Rivera was later executed by the Republican government in 1936.

1936
TIT-FOR-TAT KILLINGS

On 12 July 1936, Falange party members murdered José Castillo, a socialist and lieutenant of the Assault Guards police force. In response, the Assault Guards arrested Spanish monarchist José Calvo Sotelo the next day and executed him without trial. The events caused a round of violent reprisals and gave Nationalist generals in the Spanish army further impetus for their already-planned uprising. After their coup began on 17 July, Franco ordered his Army of Africa to rise up and secure Morocco and then attack Republican forces on the Spanish mainland.

Coup of Republican Armed Forces, July 1936.

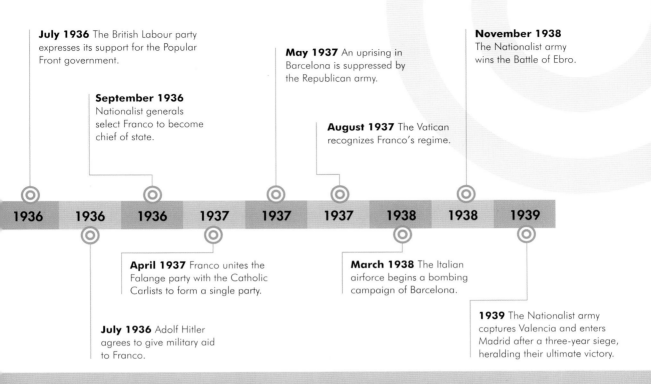

July 1936 The British Labour party expresses its support for the Popular Front government.

September 1936 Nationalist generals select Franco to become chief of state.

May 1937 An uprising in Barcelona is suppressed by the Republican army.

August 1937 The Vatican recognizes Franco's regime.

November 1938 The Nationalist army wins the Battle of Ebro.

1936	1936	1936	1937	1937	1937	1938	1938	1939

April 1937 Franco unites the Falange party with the Catholic Carlists to form a single party.

March 1938 The Italian airforce begins a bombing campaign of Barcelona.

July 1936 Adolf Hitler agrees to give military aid to Franco.

1939 The Nationalist army captures Valencia and enters Madrid after a three-year siege, heralding their ultimate victory.

1937
GUERNICA BOMBED

On 26 April 1937, aircraft from the German Condor Legion bombed the Basque town of Guernica, at Franco's behest. The Spanish Civil War was sometimes called a dress rehearsal for the Second World War: Franco received military support from fascist Italy and Germany, while the Republicans were aided by volunteers from the Soviet Union, America, Latin America and Europe. The slaughter of the unarmed citizens of Guernica by the German *Blitzkrieg* (an intense military campaign intended to bring about a swift victory) was immortalized in Pablo Picasso's *Guernica* painting, which later brought the struggle of the Republican forces to the attention of the world. The Spanish Civil War inspired other iconic artistic works, including Ernest Hemingway's novel, *For Whom the Bell Tolls*.

1938
DEFEAT AT EBRO

The Republican forces experienced heavy losses during 1937, and the area they controlled shrank substantially in 1938. The Nationalist Aragon offensive succeeded in splitting the area of Republican-held Spain in two, and an attempt to reconnect this territory in the Battle of Ebro failed in November 1938. The defeat at Ebro sealed the fate of the Republican army and Franco launched his successful invasion of Catalonia just days before the new year. By 1939, Franco had won the civil war and Nationalist celebrations were held in the cities of Spain as tanks rolled through their streets in victory.

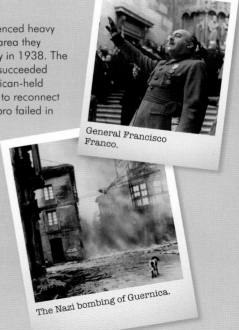

General Francisco Franco.

The Nazi bombing of Guernica.

1939
GERMANY INVADES POLAND

'...for the second time in our history a British prime minister has returned from Germany bringing peace with honour. I believe it is peace for our time.'

– British prime minister Neville Chamberlain tells Britain that giving Hitler the Sudetenland has prevented a new war in Europe

Hitler's invasion of Poland began without warning, provocation or declaration of war, and it unleashed the full force of the German army onto the militarily inferior Poles. At 4.45am on 1 September 1939, 1.5 million German soldiers supported by tanks and cavalry attacked Poland on several fronts. From 6am bombing raids commenced, as over 1,300 aircraft began their *Blitzkrieg* on Polish cities, roads and railway junctions. Towns and villages were deliberately targeted so that panicked civilians would flee their homes and block the main transport arteries. German air supremacy was achieved in a matter of hours as most of the Polish airforce was caught unawares on the ground. After the *Luftwaffe* (the German airforce) had dropped its bombs, Panzer divisions destroyed the lines of Polish defence ahead of the 62 German infantry divisions that followed behind. The Polish army, which included cavalry divisions armed with sabres, was no match for the German war machine.

By 8 September, a few Polish army strongholds remained around Pomerania, Poznan, Lodz, Krakow and Carpathia, but these were quickly bombed into submission. After only eight days of invasion, the German tanks were at the outskirts of Warsaw. A last stand in eastern Poland was called, but its success would have only been made possible with help from British and French forces, which did not arrive. The allies' promise to come to Poland's aid in the face of Nazi aggression was as worthless as its policy of appeasement towards Hitler – a policy the dictator had counted on when attacking Poland. Britain and France finally declared war on Germany on 3 September at 5pm, two days after the invasion of Poland had begun. On 17 September, all hope of Polish resistance fell when the Soviet Red Army crossed the Polish border, in fulfilment of a secret pact with Hitler. After bravely holding out for 18 days of continuous bombing, Warsaw finally surrendered on 27 September. Poland had fallen.

German troops standing in the bombed-out ruins of a Polish fort during the German invasion of Poland in the Second World War, Westerplatte, Poland.

FLASHPOINT FACT

Although Poland feared an attack by Germany, Britain and France persuaded its government not to call up its troops in August 1939, while they tried to dissuade Germany from war.

TIMELINE

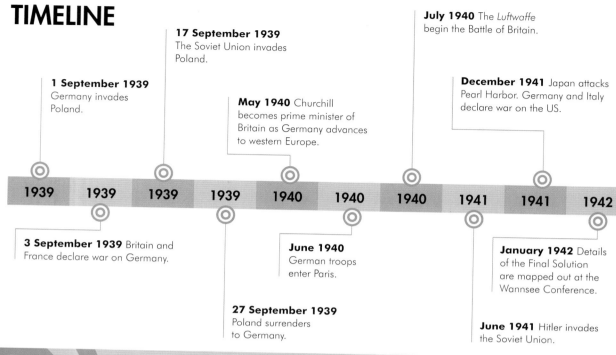

1 September 1939 Germany invades Poland.

17 September 1939 The Soviet Union invades Poland.

May 1940 Churchill becomes prime minister of Britain as Germany advances to western Europe.

July 1940 The *Luftwaffe* begin the Battle of Britain.

December 1941 Japan attacks Pearl Harbor. Germany and Italy declare war on the US.

| 1939 | 1939 | 1939 | 1939 | 1940 | 1940 | 1940 | 1941 | 1941 | 1942 |

3 September 1939 Britain and France declare war on Germany.

June 1940 German troops enter Paris.

27 September 1939 Poland surrenders to Germany.

January 1942 Details of the Final Solution are mapped out at the Wannsee Conference.

June 1941 Hitler invades the Soviet Union.

FLASHPOINTS

1936
APPEASEMENT

The First World War's Treaty of Versailles had taken away Germany's Rhineland, a strip of land that lay between France, Germany and the Low Countries (the region of northwest Europe that includes the Netherlands, Belgium and Luxembourg), which contained many industrial centres that Hitler needed to build up his military. In March 1936, in direction violation of the Treaty of Versailles, which stated that the Rhineland should remain a demilitarized zone, Hitler ordered his troops to occupy the Rhineland. Despite this breach of the treaty, neither Britain nor France mounted a response, which underlined their ineffective system of appeasement towards the Nazis.

Hitler's invasion of France began on 10 May 1940.

March 1939
SUDETENLAND

After Hitler's success in occupying the Rhineland he next targeted the Sudetenland, an area in Czechoslovakia with a large German population. The Sudetenland Germans were coaxed into staging a revolt on secret orders passed down from Hitler, who then insisted that the Sudetenland become part of Germany. Although the uprising was put down by the Czechoslovakian army, British prime minister Neville Chamberlain flew to Germany to discuss the Sudetenland with Hitler in September, 1938. After talks between Britain, France, Germany and Italy, it was agreed that Germany could have the Sudetenland on condition that it left the rest of Czechoslovakia alone. Chamberlain saw this agreement as a great victory in ensuring peace in Europe. Hitler, on the other hand, ignored the terms of the agreement and ordered his troops to enter Prague in March 1939. Czechoslovakia had become part of Germany.

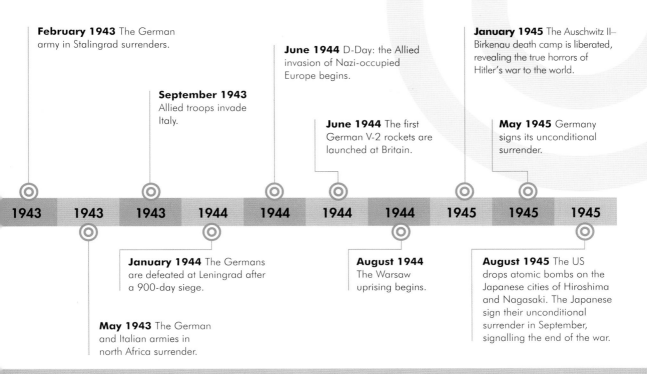

February 1943 The German army in Stalingrad surrenders.

September 1943 Allied troops invade Italy.

June 1944 D-Day: the Allied invasion of Nazi-occupied Europe begins.

June 1944 The first German V-2 rockets are launched at Britain.

January 1945 The Auschwitz II–Birkenau death camp is liberated, revealing the true horrors of Hitler's war to the world.

May 1945 Germany signs its unconditional surrender.

| 1943 | 1943 | 1943 | 1944 | 1944 | 1944 | 1944 | 1945 | 1945 | 1945 |

January 1944 The Germans are defeated at Leningrad after a 900-day siege.

August 1944 The Warsaw uprising begins.

August 1945 The US drops atomic bombs on the Japanese cities of Hiroshima and Nagasaki. The Japanese sign their unconditional surrender in September, signalling the end of the war.

May 1943 The German and Italian armies in north Africa surrender.

August 1939
STALIN PACT

In April 1939, Britain and France attempted to form a pact with Russia to come to Poland's defence if it was invaded by Germany. The terms of the agreement were not easily met: British prime minister Neville Chamberlain disliked Soviet leader Joseph Stalin, and Stalin did not trust France and Britain to stand up to Germany. Poland said it would not allow Soviet troops access through Poland to attack Germany, and the talks stalled. In the meantime, Stalin formed a secret pact with Hitler in August 1939, to attack Poland and divide it up between them. By the time the invasion of Poland began in September 1939, the country's fate had already been mapped out.

Nazi soldiers during the invasion of Poland.

1939
HOLOCAUST

After the invasion of Poland, Polish Jews were confined to ghettos and then sent to concentration camps. The first concentration camps were built in 1933, and they became the sites of mass murder where millions of people were starved, tortured, worked to death or executed. Many of the largest concentration camps were built in Nazi-occupied Poland, including Auschwitz II–Birkenau, which was designed for the mass extermination of Jews, homosexuals, Roma people and anyone else the Third Reich considered inferior. Over six million Jews were murdered in Nazi death camps, which were created to carry out Hitler's 'Final Solution' – the systematic murder of all Jews in Europe.

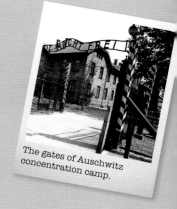

The gates of Auschwitz concentration camp.

1940—1960

The 1940s were defined by the Second World War and its terrible legacy: over 60 million people had been killed and large swathes of Europe destroyed. But the cities of Europe were not the only ones left in ruins: Japan's Hiroshima and Nagasaki had been obliterated by the first atomic bombs used in warfare. By unleashing this terrible new weapon, the United States had secured its place as one of two great superpowers to emerge from the rubble of war. The other was the Soviet Union, America's rival in the new 'Cold War' – a four-decade-long conflict fought out between the competing ideologies of communism and capitalism, without a direct blow ever being exchanged. Instead, the Cold War was waged through propaganda campaigns, the space race and proxy wars between other nations. The first of these was the Korean War, which pitted the Soviet-supported north against the US-backed south. In the end, the new People's Republic of China would lend its help to prevent North Korea's defeat by the capitalist conquerors. Like Stalin's Soviet Union, communist China showed itself to be a totalitarian regime that would sanction the deaths of millions to achieve its aims.

The ideological systems of the capitalist west, however, could also be repressive. The segregation and suppression of black people in the United States was pursued with even greater violence and vigour by South Africa's apartheid rulers. However, the civil-rights movements of both countries showed the power of popular resistance in agitating for political change. It was a lesson that would be greatly developed in the second half of the 20th century.

Profile
WINSTON CHURCHILL

Winston Churchill was one of the most influential people in British history.

Churchill was a charismatic military leader who showed his solidarity with his people by often making personal appearances alongside them.

'Let us therefore brace ourselves to our duties, and so bear ourselves that, if the British Empire and its Commonwealth last for a thousand years, men will still say, "This was their finest hour."'

– Winston Churchill delivers his 'Finest Hour' speech to the House of Commons on 18 June 1945

By May 1940, Britain and her allies were losing the war against Hitler. As the Nazis marched across Europe and one nation after another fell before the German jackboots, Britain needed a wartime prime minister to replace the weak and indecisive Neville Chamberlain. That man was Winston Churchill, the iconic leader who shone like a beacon of hope as Britain and Europe faced its darkest days. Five weeks after Churchill became prime minister, minister of defence and the leader responsible for Britain's war effort, he delivered his 'Finest Hour' speech to the nation. Churchill was famed for his rousing oratory, and his speech insisted that the people of Britain stand up and fight the Germans, as 'Hitler knows that he will have to break us in this island or lose the war.' Churchill later wrote that, at 65 years old, his moment for 'walking with destiny' had come, a moment that his previous careers as a soldier, journalist and politician had

prepared him for. Churchill's courage, spirit and energy gave inestimable inspiration to his isolated people, as France fell and his country faced the Battle of Britain and the German *Blitzkrieg* (German air raids). Hitler's defeat in the Battle of Britain ruined his plans for the invasion of Britain – 'Operation Sea Lion' – and represented a turning point in the war. Enraged, Hitler continued to try and destroy London through his Luftwaffe's *Blitzkrieg*, which destroyed over one million houses in 1940 alone. The Blitz was another defining moment for Churchill, who visited the areas reduced to rubble, often dressed in a boiler suit, to shake the hands of survivors and promise them victory was on its way. As one of the 'Big Three' Allied commanders, Churchill shaped military strategy with Stalin and Roosevelt against the Nazis and helped to redefine Europe's borders at the end of the war. Churchill was the first British statesman of the 20th century to be honoured with a state funeral.

FLASHPOINT FACT

In 1953 Churchill was awarded
the Nobel Prize for Literature.
His published works include history,
biography, war memoirs,
collected speeches and a novel.

TIMELINE

30 November 1874
Winston Leonard Spencer Churchill is born at Blenheim Palace, Oxfordshire, UK.

24 October 1900 Churchill is elected Conservative MP for Oldham and begins his parliamentary career.

22 June 1940 France surrenders to Germany, which has now overrun most of Europe.

19 February 1910 Having switched allegiance to the Liberal Party in 1904, he becomes Home Secretary in the Asquith government.

| 1874 | 1899 | 1900 | 1910 | 1939 | 1940 | 1940 |

November 1899 Working as a journalist during the Boer War, Churchill is captured but escapes on 12 December, becoming a national hero.

3 September 1939 Britain declares war on Germany. Churchill is appointed First Lord of the Admiralty in the War Cabinet.

10 May 1940 Becomes Prime Minister of an all-party coalition government, and self-appointed Minister for Defence.

FLASHPOINTS

26 May–4 June 1940
EVACUATION FROM DUNKIRK
Churchill's high-risk decision to rescue Allied troops, forced to the beaches of Dunkirk by the German advance, formed part of his determination for Britain to fight on alone. Around 338,000 men were evacuated, in what Churchill called 'a miracle of deliverance'. Reporting on this in the House of Commons, he declared, 'We shall fight on the beaches … we shall fight in the fields and in the streets … We shall never surrender.'

15 September 1940
VICTORY OVER THE LUFTWAFFE
In the summer of 1940, the Battle of Britain raged in the skies above the south coast of England and inland to London. A turning point came with a fight over the capital, in which the Luftwaffe lost 61 planes to the RAF's 31. While Churchill was visiting Fighter Command at RAF Uxbridge, Londoners watched the battle raging overhead. Germany soon abandoned daylight raids and two days later Hitler postponed his planned invasion of Britain. The selfless contribution of RAF pilots, whose average age was about 20, was summed up for all time by Churchill: 'Never, in the field of human conflict, was so much owed by so many to so few.'

Aircraft over London during the Battle of Britain

British evacuation from Dunkirk, France, World War II

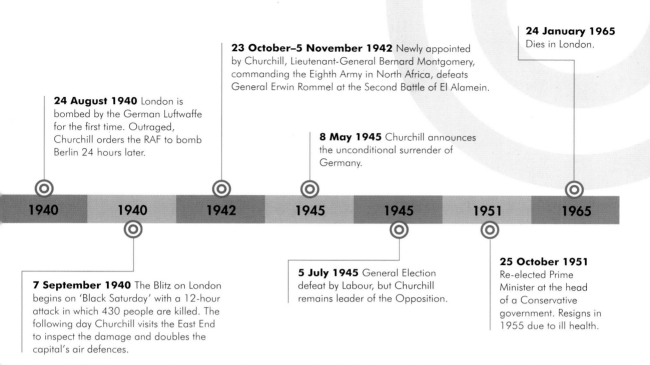

24 January 1965 Dies in London.

23 October–5 November 1942 Newly appointed by Churchill, Lieutenant-General Bernard Montgomery, commanding the Eighth Army in North Africa, defeats General Erwin Rommel at the Second Battle of El Alamein.

24 August 1940 London is bombed by the German Luftwaffe for the first time. Outraged, Churchill orders the RAF to bomb Berlin 24 hours later.

8 May 1945 Churchill announces the unconditional surrender of Germany.

1940	1940	1942	1945	1945	1951	1965

7 September 1940 The Blitz on London begins on 'Black Saturday' with a 12-hour attack in which 430 people are killed. The following day Churchill visits the East End to inspect the damage and doubles the capital's air defences.

5 July 1945 General Election defeat by Labour, but Churchill remains leader of the Opposition.

25 October 1951 Re-elected Prime Minister at the head of a Conservative government. Resigns in 1955 due to ill health.

14 August 1941
ATLANTIC CHARTER

Against the backdrop of Fascist tyranny, Churchill met Roosevelt in Placentia Bay, Newfoundland, to construct a set of principles for a peaceful postwar world. This document, signed by both, was called the Atlantic Charter and was formally adopted at the founding of the United Nations Organization in San Francisco, in 1945. Its principles included the right of nations to safety and sovereignty, and of all citizens to live in 'freedom from fear and want'.

Franklin D. Roosevelt pictured here in January 1943.

14–24 January 1943
CONFERENCE IN CASABLANCA

Two months after the Anglo-American landings in North Africa, Churchill met President Roosevelt to co-ordinate plans for victory over the Axis powers (Germany, Italy and Japan). It was the first of several such conferences. Churchill prevailed with his aim of completing the German defeat in North Africa, to be followed by an invasion of Sicily. Both agreed to postpone D-Day to the following year, but meanwhile to deliver aid to the Soviet Union and conduct a major bombing campaign of German cities.

1945

HIROSHIMA

*'The atom bomb was no "great decision".
It was merely another powerful weapon in
the arsenal of righteousness.'*

– US president Harry S. Truman speaks about the atomic bombs he ordered
to be dropped on Japan during the Second World War

At 8.15am on 6 August 1945, the United States dropped 'the most terrible bomb in the history of the world' on the Japanese city of Hiroshima. The first atomic bomb ever used in warfare was delivered by B-29 bomber the *Enola Gay* and exploded in a blinding flash of light 580m (1,902ft) above the ground. From its point of impact, the bomb destroyed over 16 sq km (6 sq miles) of the city and produced a wave of heat so intense that many people were simply vaporized where they stood. Between 60,000 and 80,000 people were killed instantly in the bomb blast. The initial blast was followed by violent winds that caused a series of firestorms to rage for three days throughout the remains of the city. Thousands of people who had survived the explosion were killed in the fires that followed it. Those who were left alive tried to flee the city, but many later succumbed to their injuries and the radiation

Colonel Paul Tibbets stands in front of the *Enola Gay*, the B-29 bomber he picked out to drop the bomb on Hiroshima and named after his mother.

sickness caused by exposure to the bomb. In the end, Hiroshima's death toll stood at 135,000. Hiroshima had been chosen as a target by US president Harry S. Truman because it had not previously been bombed during America's raids on Japan. It therefore provided an unscarred model that would show the full damage that an atomic weapon could inflict on a city. America had used the atomic bomb because it feared that a ground invasion of Japan would cause an even greater loss of life. It hoped Japan would quickly agree to an unconditional surrender after experiencing America's destructive new weapon and thus bring an end to the Second World War. However, three days after Hiroshima, the Japanese government had made no move to surrender. In response, the US dropped another atomic bomb on the city of Nagasaki. The Japanese surrendered shortly afterwards, on 2 September 1945. The Second World War was officially over.

ENOLA GAY

NO S...

TIMELINE

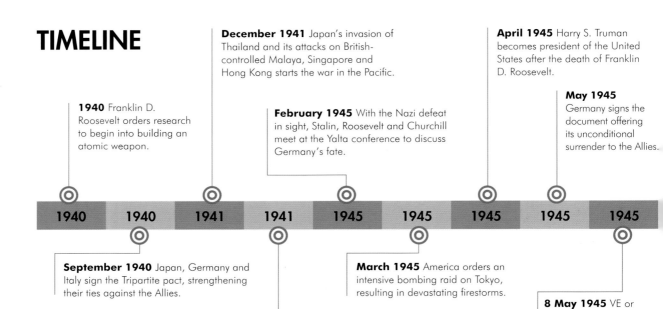

1940 Franklin D. Roosevelt orders research to begin into building an atomic weapon.

December 1941 Japan's invasion of Thailand and its attacks on British-controlled Malaya, Singapore and Hong Kong starts the war in the Pacific.

February 1945 With the Nazi defeat in sight, Stalin, Roosevelt and Churchill meet at the Yalta conference to discuss Germany's fate.

April 1945 Harry S. Truman becomes president of the United States after the death of Franklin D. Roosevelt.

May 1945 Germany signs the document offering its unconditional surrender to the Allies.

| 1940 | 1940 | 1941 | 1941 | 1945 | 1945 | 1945 | 1945 | 1945 |

September 1940 Japan, Germany and Italy sign the Tripartite pact, strengthening their ties against the Allies.

March 1945 America orders an intensive bombing raid on Tokyo, resulting in devastating firestorms.

December 1941 Japan attacks the Pearl Harbor US naval base in Hawaii, bringing America into the war.

8 May 1945 VE or 'Victory in Europe' day is celebrated in the cities of Europe.

FLASHPOINTS

1942
THE MANHATTAN PROJECT

In 1939, Albert Einstein wrote to US president Franklin D. Roosevelt to tell him that developments in nuclear physics had opened the way for the design of an atomic weapon. Roosevelt immediately ordered a top-secret military programme to create the bomb, which would give the Allied powers an unstoppable advantage over Germany. The resulting programme became the 'Manhattan' in 1942 and it included top physicists from Allied countries around the world. After the programme was able to successfully create a bomb, new US president Harry S. Truman wrote in his diary, 'We have discovered the most terrible bomb in the history of the world.' The two bombs the scientists built – Little Boy and Fat Man – caused massive loss of life, the end of the Second World War and the beginning of a new, nuclear age.

March 1945
BOMBING JAPAN

As increasing Allied victories over Germany drew the war in Europe to a close, Japan showed no signs of ending its hostilities. To bomb the country into submission, the US dropped over 2,000 tonnes of incendiary bombs on Tokyo on 9 March 1945. The bombs created vast firestorms that destroyed almost 41 sq km (16 sq miles) of the Japanese capital and killed between 80,000 and 130,000 civilians. The stench of burning human flesh was reportedly so strong that the American bomber pilots were forced to wear oxygen masks to stop them from vomiting as they delivered their payloads over the city.

The familiar mushroom cloud of a nuclear blast.

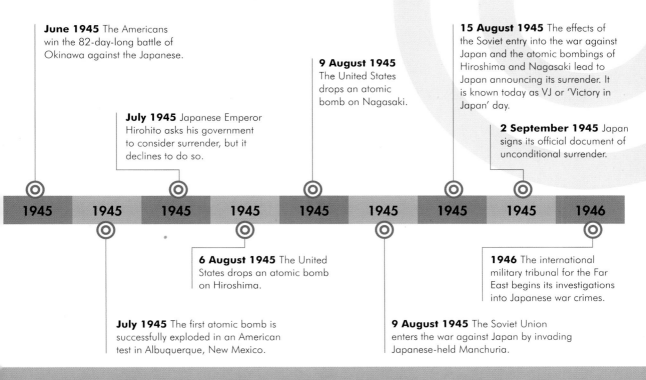

June 1945 The Americans win the 82-day-long battle of Okinawa against the Japanese.

July 1945 Japanese Emperor Hirohito asks his government to consider surrender, but it declines to do so.

9 August 1945 The United States drops an atomic bomb on Nagasaki.

15 August 1945 The effects of the Soviet entry into the war against Japan and the atomic bombings of Hiroshima and Nagasaki lead to Japan announcing its surrender. It is known today as VJ or 'Victory in Japan' day.

2 September 1945 Japan signs its official document of unconditional surrender.

| 1945 | 1945 | 1945 | 1945 | 1945 | 1945 | 1945 | 1945 | 1946 |

6 August 1945 The United States drops an atomic bomb on Hiroshima.

1946 The international military tribunal for the Far East begins its investigations into Japanese war crimes.

July 1945 The first atomic bomb is successfully exploded in an American test in Albuquerque, New Mexico.

9 August 1945 The Soviet Union enters the war against Japan by invading Japanese-held Manchuria.

July–August 1945
THE POTSDAM CONFERENCE
After the war in Europe had ended, US president Harry S. Truman met British prime minister Winston Churchill and Soviet leader Joseph Stalin at the Potsdam Conference in July 1945. The conference was designed to redraw Europe's borders and also discuss what to do about Japan. At the end of July, the Allies issued a declaration to Japan asking it to surrender or otherwise face 'utter destruction'. Unaware of America's new atomic capabilities, Japan decided not to comply with the threat.

September 1945
JAPAN SURRENDERS
On 2 September 1945, Japan signed the official document detailing its unconditional surrender. It followed the devastating 'Fat Boy' bomb being dropped on the city of Nagasaki on 9 August. Although the bomb was more powerful than the 'Little Boy' dropped on Hiroshima, the impact of the blast was partially contained by the hills surrounding the city. Despite this, between 40,000 and 80,000 people were killed by the explosion. Even after the devastation of Hiroshima and Nagasaki, the Japanese government was still divided on whether to surrender. However, Emperor Hirohito intervened to prevent any more loss of Japanese life. When Hirohito made a radio announcement on 15 August that Japan would surrender, it was the first time many people had heard his voice. Hiroshima was later rebuilt as a peace memorial.

Final preparations on the 'Little Boy' bomb.

The flattened city of Hiroshima following the bomb blast.

1948

APARTHEID INTRODUCED IN SOUTH AFRICA

'There is no place for [the Bantu] in the European community above the level of certain forms of labour.'

– South African prime minister Hendrik Verwoerd explains why he considered educating black South Africans to be pointless

Racial segregation and the supremacy of white governments had dominated South African life long before apartheid began. It had started three years after South Africa gained its independence, when the 1913 Natives Land Act reserved the majority of South African land for whites only. Black South Africans, who made up 67 per cent of the population, were now only allowed to buy land in barren reserves. Apartheid, or 'apart-hood' was introduced by the all-white National party after it was elected into government in 1948. The party wasted no time in enacting its apartheid policies that would relegate blacks to a life of servitude by law. The 1949 Prohibition of Mixed Marriages Act banned mixed marriages and the 1950 Immorality Act made sexual relations between blacks and whites illegal. The 1950 Population Registration Act then classified all South Africans as black, white, coloured or Indian. A person's racial classification was sometimes established by the 'pencil test', which involved pushing a pencil through a person's hair to determine its 'Afro-texture'. Black South African children were then prepared for adult lives as labourers and servants through the 1953 Bantu Education Act, which created a separate education system for blacks. From 1950 to 1953, South Africa became increasingly segregated, with the creation of separate public transport, schools and hospitals, and signboards designating 'whites-only' areas. In 1958, prime minister H.F. Verwoerd introduced the forced removal of 3.5 million black Africans to 'homelands' – large, over-populated slums without proper infrastructure that served as migrant labour pools for white employers. Blacks were then forced by law to carry identity passbooks, called *dompas*, when outside their homelands. The racist policies of the National Party were opposed by a group of young idealists including the leader of the African National Congress, Nelson Mandela, whose work led to the overthrow of apartheid in 1994.

Black South Africans protest against their government's apartheid rule, a policy of racial segregation that lasted for 36 years.

FLASHPOINT FACT

Many people in the west boycotted South African products such as fruit and wine during apartheid, in protest at its racist rule.

TIMELINE

1881 The Boers (farmers mainly of Dutch ancestry) rebel against the British, which sparks the first Anglo-Boer War.

1902 The second Anglo-Boer War ends with the Treaty of Vereeniging. The Transvaal and Orange Free State are made self-governing colonies of Britain.

1912 The South African Native National Congress is formed, later to become the African National Congress (ANC).

1915 The South African National party is founded.

1934 The Status of the Union Act is passed, declaring South Africa 'a sovereign independent state'.

1950 The Group Areas Act segregates blacks and whites and bans the Communist party. The ANC responds with a campaign of civil disobedience.

1881	1899	1902	1910	1912	1913	1915	1931	1934	1948	1950	1958

1910 The formation of the union of South Africa.

1899 The second Boer War begins when British soldiers amass on the Transvaal border.

1931 Britain passes the Statute of Westminster, which removes British legal authority over South Africa.

1913 The Natives Land Act is introduced to prevent black South Africans from buying land outside reserves.

1958 Hendrik Verwoerd is elected prime minister of South Africa.

1948 Apartheid is formally adopted by prime minister D.F. Malan, following the National Party's election to power.

FLASHPOINTS

1913
THE NATIVES LANDS ACT

In 1910, the Union of South Africa was formed from the unification of British colonies the Cape Colony, Natal, Transvaal and the Orange River. The next few years became pivotal to the future political landscape of the newly established South Africa. In 1912 the South African Native National Congress was founded – later to become the African National Congress (ANC), the party that would fight and eventually overcome South Africa's apartheid rule. In 1913, the Natives Land Act laid the groundwork for the introduction of apartheid. The Land Act restricted the ownership of land for black South Africans to just seven per cent of agricultural land, which was laid out in reserves. Blacks were also forbidden from working as tenants on white-owned land or buying and leasing land outside the reserves, except from other black Africans. The Act had a devastating impact on the country's large number of black sharecroppers and labour tenants.

1950
THE GROUP AREAS ACT

The Group Areas Act segregated South Africa into separate areas for whites and blacks. Blacks were forbidden from living in the more developed white areas and were therefore often forced to commute for long distances from their homes to work. The law also required that blacks had to carry 'passbooks', a type of internal passport, when they entered white parts of the country, and allowed them to be forcibly removed if they were found in the wrong area. The 1950 Group Areas Act led to opposition from the African National Congress and its leader Nelson Mandela, who organized a campaign of civil disobedience in response.

SLEGS BLANKES EUROPEANS ONLY.

A black person illegally occupies a space for whites only.

1960 Sixty-nine black demonstrators are killed and 180 injured in the Sharpeville Massacre. The ANC is banned by the government.

1961 South Africa is declared a republic and leaves the Commonwealth. Nelson Mandela heads up the ANC's new military wing, which launches a campaign of sabotage.

1966 South African prime minister Hendrik Verwoerd is assassinated.

1976 Over 600 people are killed in clashes between black protesters and security forces during the Soweto uprising.

1991 Multi-party talks begin. Prime minister F.W. de Klerk repeals the remaining apartheid laws and international sanctions are lifted.

1999 The ANC wins general elections and Thabo Mbeki becomes president.

1960	1960s	1961	1964	1966	1970s	1976	1990	1991	1994	1999	2013

1964 Nelson Mandela is sentenced to life imprisonment.

1990 The ANC is unbanned and Nelson Mandela is released after 27 years in prison.

2013 Nelson Mandela dies at the age of 95.

1960s South Africa is excluded from the Olympic Games following international pressure on its government.

1970s Three and a half million people are forcibly resettled in black homelands.

1994 The ANC wins the first non-racial elections and Nelson Mandela becomes president of South Africa.

1960
THE SHARPEVILLE MASSACRE
On 21 March 1960, police fired on a crowd of protestors and killed 69 people in what became known as the Sharpeville Massacre. The peaceful march had been organized in the Transvaal township of Sharpeville by the Pan-African Congress (PAC) to protest against South Africa's Pass Laws. The Pass Laws required all black people to carry a passbook when moving outside their designated black homeland areas. As the protestors approached the police station, members of the police panicked and began firing. The massacre sparked subsequent protests by the PAC and ANC that were sharply repressed and both parties were banned by the government.

1962
INTERNATIONAL PRESSURE
The United Nations became critical of South Africa's policy of apartheid following the Sharpeville Massacre of 1960. The UN's Security Council called for an end to policies of racial separation and, in 1962, the UN General Assembly passed Resolution 1761, which condemned South Africa's apartheid outright. International military embargoes and economic sanctions followed, but these did not produce an immediate effect. In 1961, South Africa severed more of its colonial ties by becoming a republic and withdrawing from its place in the Commonwealth. As South Africa looked immune from international pressure, Nelson Mandela took a more militant approach to opposing the government. This would lead to Mandela's arrest in 1964 and a 27-year imprisonment for treason.

The 1960 Sharpeville Massacre.

Protestors from around the world call for Mandela's release.

1950
THE KOREAN WAR BEGINS

General Douglas MacArthur led the United Nations forces in the Korean War.

'It seems strangely difficult for some to realize that here in Asia is where the communist conspirators have elected to make their play for global conquest, and that we have joined the issue thus raised on the battlefield.'

– A letter from General Douglas MacArthur, 1951

On 25 June 1950, around 100,000 North Korean soldiers poured across the 38th parallel into South Korea and began the Korean War. The war would often be fought by proxy between the two superpowers – the Soviet Union and the United States – and their competing ideologies: capitalism against communism. Korea had been divided during the Second World War into the Soviet-controlled north, which became the People's Democratic Republic of Korea, and the US-controlled south, which became the Republic of Korea. The boundary separating the country became known as the 38th parallel. Although the two Korean governments of the north and south were formed in 1948, both the US and the Soviet Union retained their influence. North Korea's invasion of the south was carried out with Soviet weaponry and had Stalin's blessing. The United Nations Security Council, however, condemned the invasion and called for its members to assist South Korea in a 'police action' against the aggressors. On 27 June, president Harry S. Truman authorized the US military to engage North Korea under the command of General Douglas MacArthur. On 15 September, a combined force of South Korean and US troops – who made up nearly 90 per cent of the UN military force on the ground – launched a counter-offensive against the North Korean army. The initial results were poor, but after an amphibious assault at the Battle of Inchon, the Americans liberated Seoul from the North Koreans and forced them into a retreat. Victory seemed at hand when MacArthur was able to push the Northern Korean army as far north as the Chinese border. However, this was the moment that the People's Republic of China joined the war for North Korea, which prolonged the war until 1953. Although an armistice ended the fighting in the same year, the Cold War that the Korean conflict had ignited would go on for another four decades.

Members of the US 187th Airborne Regimental Combat Team drop into North Korean territory to cut off the connecting road with China.

FLASHPOINT FACT

The Korean War never officially ended. The two countries are still divided today by the same 3-km (2-mile) wide demilitarized zone that was put in place in 1953.

TIMELINE

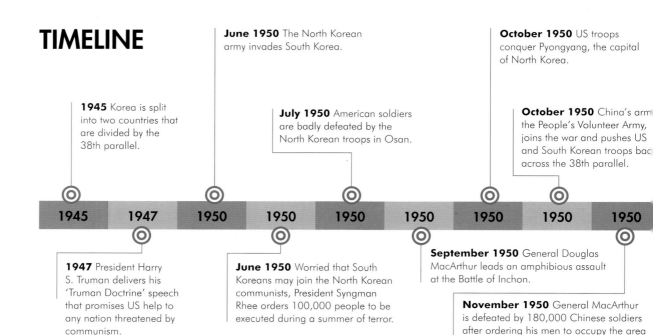

June 1950 The North Korean army invades South Korea.

October 1950 US troops conquer Pyongyang, the capital of North Korea.

1945 Korea is split into two countries that are divided by the 38th parallel.

July 1950 American soldiers are badly defeated by the North Korean troops in Osan.

October 1950 China's arm the People's Volunteer Army, joins the war and pushes US and South Korean troops bac across the 38th parallel.

| 1945 | 1947 | 1950 | 1950 | 1950 | 1950 | 1950 | 1950 | 1950 |

1947 President Harry S. Truman delivers his 'Truman Doctrine' speech that promises US help to any nation threatened by communism.

June 1950 Worried that South Koreans may join the North Korean communists, President Syngman Rhee orders 100,000 people to be executed during a summer of terror.

September 1950 General Douglas MacArthur leads an amphibious assault at the Battle of Inchon.

November 1950 General MacArthur is defeated by 180,000 Chinese soldiers after ordering his men to occupy the area around the Yalu river, the border between North Korea and China.

FLASHPOINTS

1945
FOREIGN-BACKED KOREA

From 1910 until 1945, Korea was under Japanese rule. Then, after the end of the war in Europe, the Soviet Union declared war on Japan and invaded northern Korea as part of an agreement with the United States. The US then occupied the area of Korea south of the 38th parallel. Shortly afterwards, Japan surrendered. By 1948, communist leader Kim Il-sung had established the People's Democratic Republic of Korea and the Republic of Korea was formed in the south. The governments were backed by the Soviet Union and United States respectively.

1950
SOUTHERN FIGHTBACK

After the North Korean invasion of the south in June, UN members from 15 nations sent troops to help. By July, American bombers were making raids behind the North Korean lines, which helped bring the advancing army to a halt. The ensuing fightback at the Battle of Inchon saw the retreat of the North Korean army and turned the tide of the war. General MacArthur met with President Truman in September 1950 to tell him that the North Korean army had been defeated. His proclamation was premature, however, as two weeks later the Chinese joined the side of the North Koreans.

North Korean leader, Kim Il-sung.

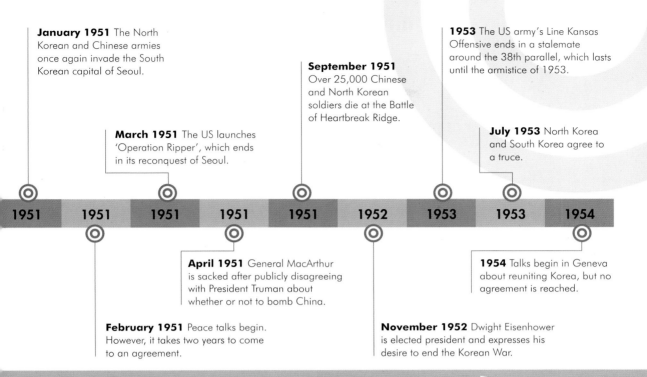

January 1951 The North Korean and Chinese armies once again invade the South Korean capital of Seoul.

March 1951 The US launches 'Operation Ripper', which ends in its reconquest of Seoul.

September 1951 Over 25,000 Chinese and North Korean soldiers die at the Battle of Heartbreak Ridge.

1953 The US army's Line Kansas Offensive ends in a stalemate around the 38th parallel, which lasts until the armistice of 1953.

July 1953 North Korea and South Korea agree to a truce.

1951	1951	1951	1951	1951	1952	1953	1953	1954

April 1951 General MacArthur is sacked after publicly disagreeing with President Truman about whether or not to bomb China.

1954 Talks begin in Geneva about reuniting Korea, but no agreement is reached.

February 1951 Peace talks begin. However, it takes two years to come to an agreement.

November 1952 Dwight Eisenhower is elected president and expresses his desire to end the Korean War.

1951
MACARTHUR FIRED

In April, President Truman relieved General MacArthur as supreme US commander in Korea and replaced him with General Matthew Ridgway. MacArthur's dismissal occurred for several reasons. Firstly, he had wrongly promised Truman that China would not join the war. When this did happen it led to heavy US casualties, after Americans troops crossed the 38th parallel in pursuit of the retreating North Korean army. MacArthur then became determined to invade China and advocated the use of nuclear weapons to win the war. Truman disagreed with MacArthur, believing that withdrawal from Korea would be a better outcome than an ongoing Asian land war. MacArthur was also criticized for not actually setting foot in Korea and instead conducting the Korean War from the safety of Japan.

1953
ARMISTICE

From July 1951, commanders from North and South Korea began peace talks. Both sides were willing to accept a ceasefire that would maintain the division of the two nations along the boundary line of the 38th parallel. However, consensus could not be reached on the fate of their prisoners of war (POWs), and the Korean War lasted for another two years as negotiations continued. In the end, the two sides signed an armistice on 27 July 1953. The terms of the agreement allowed the POWs from both sides to stay where they pleased and also created a 3-km (2-mile) wide 'demilitarized zone' along the 38th parallel border.

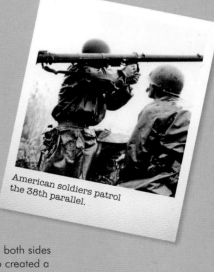

American soldiers patrol the 38th parallel.

1953

HILLARY CONQUERS EVEREST

New Zealander Edmund Hillary was the first man to conquer Everest.

'Well, George, we knocked the bastard off.'

– Edmund Hillary's first words to his climbing companion and lifelong friend George Lowe after conquering Everest

A photograph of Edmund Hillary mountaineering. Although there is a photo of Tenzing Norgay on the summit of Everest, Hillary declined having his picture taken.

As Edmund Hillary and Tenzing Norgay set foot on the summit of Everest, they gave each other a polite handshake – and then a joyful embrace. The New Zealand climber and his Nepalese Sherpa guide had just achieved what no other man had before: the ascent of the 8,848-m (29,021-ft) high Mount Everest, the highest point on the planet. Hillary and Tenzing had set out ten weeks earlier as part of the 1953 British Everest Expedition led by Colonel John Hunt. The expedition, which included 362 porters, 20 Sherpa guides, a *Times* reporter and five tonnes of supplies, trekked for 274km (170 miles) from Kathmandu, Nepal, to the village of Namche Bazaar, which they reached on 10 March. After three days of training, the expedition made its way to Mount Everest's base camp and then worked its way up the mountain's South Col. After the climbers pitched a base camp at 7,890m (25,879ft),

Tom Bourdillon and Charles Evans made an attempt on the summit. The pair came within 91m (298ft) of the top, but had to turn back when Evans' oxygen system failed. Hunt then ordered Hillary and Tenzing to try for the top. The climbers set out on 26 May and pitched a last tent 8,500m (27,880ft) above sea level. In the morning Hillary's boots were frozen solid, and he had to warm them up before the final ascent. The last hurdle between the climbers and the top was a 12-m (39-ft) rock face, now known as the 'Hillary Step'. Hillary negotiated the cliff by inching himself up a crack in the rock and then hauling Tenzing up behind him. After reaching the summit at 11.30am on 29 May, the pair took photographs, planted the flags of Britain, Nepal, the United Nations and India, and Norgay buried some sweets in the snow as a Buddhist offering. After 15 minutes, with their oxygen supply running low, the climbers began their descent back down the mountain.

FLASHPOINT FACT

Everest sits on the Nepal–Tibet border and was named after British surveyor George Everest. It is known in Tibet as Chomolungma, or 'Goddess Mother of the World'.

TIMELINE

1922 The first attempt to reach the summit of Mount Everest fails, although members of the British expedition become the first humans to climb above 8,000m (26,240ft).

1933 A British expedition to Everest's summit fails and climber Percy Wyn-Harris declares it 'unclimbable'.

1935 Tenzing Norgay makes his first visit to Everest, as a porter employed for a British reconnaissance mission.

1947 Canadian Earl Denman enters Tibet illegally and is then defeated in his attempt on Everest.

1951 British climbers including Eric Shipton, Edmu Hillary and Tom Bourdillon survey Everest's southern fac

| 1922 | 1924 | 1933 | 1934 | 1935 | 1938 | 1947 | 1950 | 1951 | 1952 |

1924 British climbers George Mallory and Andrew Irvine are seen for the last time during their Everest ascent. Mallory's body was found in 1999.

1938 Explorer Bill Tilman reaches 8,290m (27,191ft) without supplemental oxygen for the first time.

1952 A Swiss expedition becomes the first to reach the Western Cwm.

1934 British eccentric Maurice Wilson dies during an attempt on Everest.

1950 Nepal opens its borders to foreigners, making the easier southern route up the mountain accessible.

FLASHPOINTS

1935
MOUNTAINEER BEGINNINGS

At 16 years old, Edmund Hillary was a gangly and uncoordinated teenager who spent his spare time reading books. But on a class trip to Mount Ruapehu in New Zealand's North Island, Hillary discovered a love for climbing. As an adult he took up an occupation as a beekeeper, which allowed him to climb New Zealand's mountain ranges during the winter. In 1948, Hillary made a successful ascent of Aoraki, also known as Mount Cook, which is New Zealand's highest peak at 3,754m (12,313ft) above sea level.

The 1953 British Everest Expedition begins its ascent.

1951
EVEREST EXPEDITION

In 1951, a British expedition travelled to Everest to establish a route up the mountain via its southern face. The expedition members, which included Eric Shipton, Tom Bourdillon and Edmund Hillary, surveyed the mountain's Western Cym valley and concluded it would be possible to traverse through it and then onto the South Col. From the South Col an attempt on the summit could be mounted. The climbers spent the next month attempting to reach the Western Cwm through the Khumbu Icefall, but were defeated at the last hurdle – an impassable, 30-m (98-ft) wide crevasse.

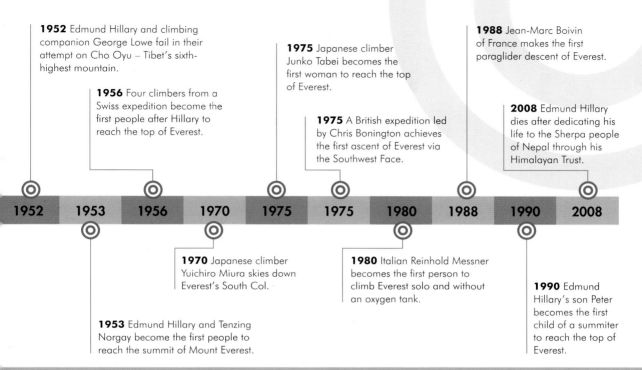

1952 Edmund Hillary and climbing companion George Lowe fail in their attempt on Cho Oyu – Tibet's sixth-highest mountain.

1956 Four climbers from a Swiss expedition become the first people after Hillary to reach the top of Everest.

1975 Japanese climber Junko Tabei becomes the first woman to reach the top of Everest.

1975 A British expedition led by Chris Bonington achieves the first ascent of Everest via the Southwest Face.

1988 Jean-Marc Boivin of France makes the first paraglider descent of Everest.

2008 Edmund Hillary dies after dedicating his life to the Sherpa people of Nepal through his Himalayan Trust.

| 1952 | 1953 | 1956 | 1970 | 1975 | 1975 | 1980 | 1988 | 1990 | 2008 |

1970 Japanese climber Yuichiro Miura skies down Everest's South Col.

1980 Italian Reinhold Messner becomes the first person to climb Everest solo and without an oxygen tank.

1990 Edmund Hillary's son Peter becomes the first child of a summiter to reach the top of Everest.

1953 Edmund Hillary and Tenzing Norgay become the first people to reach the summit of Mount Everest.

1953
EVEREST NEWSFLASH
News reached London on 2 June 1953 that Hillary and Tenzing of the British Everest Expedition had conquered the mountain. *Times* reporter James Morris had sent the news from Mount Everest in a coded message that was taken to the village of Namche Bazaar in Nepal by a runner. The message was then relayed to London via a wireless transmitter. By the time Hillary returned to Kathmandu a few days later, it was to the news that he had been knighted. Intense media interest followed and everyone wanted to know who had stepped foot on the summit first. Tenzing later said that it had been Hillary.

The newspapers report Hillary's success.

1996
CONQUESTS AND DEATHS
Over the years following Hillary and Tenzing's conquest of Everest, dozens of people from different countries were able to emulate their accomplishment. Notable firsts included the first person to reach the summit without oxygen, the first woman to reach the top and the first person to climb Everest solo. However, amidst criticism that climbing the mountain had become too commercial, came one of the most lethal years in Everest's history. In May 1996, eight people died trying to reach the top of Everest when they were caught in a blizzard. Four more died later that year, also trying to reach the summit. Everest would claim 16 further victims during an avalanche in 2014, and another 19 died in 2015, during an avalanche caused by the Nepal earthquakes of that year.

Mount Everest is located in the Mahalangur section of the Himalayas.

1955
ROSA PARKS' BUS PROTEST

'I'd see the bus pass every day…but to me, that was a way of life; we had no choice but to accept what was the custom. The bus was among the first ways I realized there was a black world and a white world.'

– Rosa Parks remembers seeing the bus for white children drive past as she walked to school

Rosa Parks seemed like an ordinary Montgomery seamstress going about her everyday life when she boarded her bus home on 1 December 1955. But through a simple and quiet moment of civil disobedience, she was about to change history. Buses in Alabama at that time were segregated into sections for whites and blacks, and Parks sat down just behind the ten seats reserved for whites. When the bus filled with white people, Parks was obliged to move – but she refused to stand up. The bus driver threatened to call the police, and then did so when this did not have the desired effect. Parks was duly arrested, fingerprinted and charged with violating the segregation laws, commonly known as the 'Jim Crow Laws'. Parks appealed against her conviction and challenged the legality of segregation under the American Constitution. As she did so, little-known civil rights leader Martin Luther King, Jr. initiated a boycott of Montgomery buses by black

Rosa Parks rides a Montgomery bus on 21 December 1956, the day the city's public transportation system became integrated.

Americans, who made up around 70 per cent of its passengers. Nearly a year later, on 13 November 1956, the US Supreme Court upheld a lower court's decision that Montgomery's segregated buses were unconstitutional. A court order to this effect was served the next day and the bus boycott officially ended on 20 December. The ruling was a monumental moment in American history that ignited the civil-rights movement across the country. The boycott brought Martin Luther King, Jr. to prominence and made Rosa Parks famous as the 'mother of the civil-rights movement'. Parks was not viewed with the same admiration by her employers. She was fired from her job and had to leave Montgomery after being unable to obtain work. She was later employed as a secretary for a US congressman in Michigan and co-founded the Rosa and Raymond Parks Institute for Self Development, which gave career advice to young people.

FLASHPOINT FACT

Rosa Parks was not careful with
her money and gave much of
it away to civil-rights causes.
After being threatened with eviction
from her apartment for non-payment
of rent, the building owners
decided to let her live there
rent free until her death in 2005.

TIMELINE

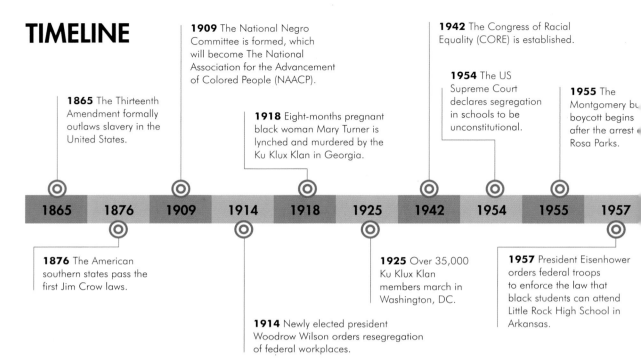

1909 The National Negro Committee is formed, which will become The National Association for the Advancement of Colored People (NAACP).

1865 The Thirteenth Amendment formally outlaws slavery in the United States.

1918 Eight-months pregnant black woman Mary Turner is lynched and murdered by the Ku Klux Klan in Georgia.

1942 The Congress of Racial Equality (CORE) is established.

1954 The US Supreme Court declares segregation in schools to be unconstitutional.

1955 The Montgomery bu boycott begins after the arrest Rosa Parks.

| 1865 | 1876 | 1909 | 1914 | 1918 | 1925 | 1942 | 1954 | 1955 | 1957 |

1876 The American southern states pass the first Jim Crow laws.

1925 Over 35,000 Ku Klux Klan members march in Washington, DC.

1957 President Eisenhower orders federal troops to enforce the law that black students can attend Little Rock High School in Arkansas.

1914 Newly elected president Woodrow Wilson orders resegregation of federal workplaces.

FLASHPOINTS

1955
BUS BOYCOTT BEGINS

On 5 December 1955 – four days after Rosa Parks was arrested – a black boycott of Montgomery buses was called for. Members of the National Association for the Advancement of Colored People (NAACP) handed out tens of thousands of handbills, church leaders told their congregations to stay off the buses and a front-page article in the *Montgomery Advertiser* spread the word around Montgomery. It was agreed that black people would stay off the buses until segregation had been removed, black drivers had been hired and black people were treated with same courtesy on buses as whites. Over 40,000 black commuters stayed off the buses the next morning, choosing to walk, ride in carpools or travel in black-operated cabs that charged them ten cents – the same fare as on the bus.

1960
THE GREENSBORO FOUR

Following the civil disobedience sparked by the Montgomery bus boycott, four university students staged a sit-in at a Woolworths store in Greensboro, North Carolina. After shopping at Woolworths, the university men were refused service at the store's segregated lunch counter. Despite being asked to leave, the four students stayed at the counter until the store closed. The next day, over 20 black students staged another sit-in, and the following day over 60 more. The protest soon spread to other towns in North Carolina and then the neighbouring states of Mississippi, Virginia, Kentucky and Tennessee. The protests proved to be a pivotal moment in the American civil-rights movement and led to President Dwight D. Eisenhower expressing his sympathy for the cause. The Greensboro Woolworths store changed its segregation policy soon afterwards.

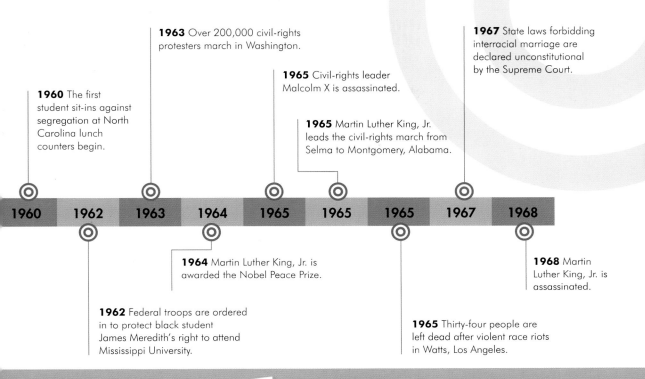

1960 The first student sit-ins against segregation at North Carolina lunch counters begin.

1963 Over 200,000 civil-rights protesters march in Washington.

1965 Civil-rights leader Malcolm X is assassinated.

1965 Martin Luther King, Jr. leads the civil-rights march from Selma to Montgomery, Alabama.

1967 State laws forbidding interracial marriage are declared unconstitutional by the Supreme Court.

| 1960 | 1962 | 1963 | 1964 | 1965 | 1965 | 1965 | 1967 | 1968 |

1964 Martin Luther King, Jr. is awarded the Nobel Peace Prize.

1968 Martin Luther King, Jr. is assassinated.

1962 Federal troops are ordered in to protect black student James Meredith's right to attend Mississippi University.

1965 Thirty-four people are left dead after violent race riots in Watts, Los Angeles.

1963
I HAVE A DREAM

On 28 August 1962, over 200,000 protestors gathered for a civil-rights rally known as 'the March on Washington for Jobs and Freedom'. The march was designed to draw attention to the growing dissatisfaction over black discrimination in America, and culminated in Martin Luther King, Jr.'s 'I Have a Dream' speech, which called for economic and political equality. In addition to Martin Luther King, Jr., the march included performances by Joan Baez and Bob Dylan and was broadcast live on television, which brought great publicity to the civil-rights cause.

Martin Luther King, Jr addresses his followers.

1964
THE CIVIL RIGHTS ACT

From the mid-1960s, the American federal government passed a number of laws banning racial discrimination in the United States: the Civil Rights Act of 1964 outlawed discrimination based on race, colour, religion, sex or national origin; the Voting Rights Act of 1965 prohibited racial discrimination in voting; and the Fair Housing Act of 1968 made it illegal to discriminate racially when selling or renting property. While serious issues concerning racial inequality remain in America to the present day, the civil-rights movement that had been ignited by Rosa Parks in 1955 was pivotal in securing equal rights by law.

A civil-rights protest in the late 1950s.

1957
USSR LAUNCHES *SPUTNIK*

'The Soviet Union has become the seacoast of the universe.'

– Chief Soviet rocket engineer and spacecraft designer Sergei Korolev on his country's space-race achievements

On 4 October 1957, the Soviet Union stunned the world by launching the first satellite into orbit. *Sputnik 1* was an 84-kg (186-lb) steel ball that reached a speed of around 28,164kph (17,500mph) and circled the earth every 96.17 minutes. Built with four radio antennae, *Sputnik* sent back information about the Earth's atmosphere via distinctive 'beeps'. These could be heard by radio transmitters in both Britain and the United States, proving that *Sputnik* was more than just a wishful Soviet propaganda story. News of the satellite both amazed and horrified the United States government. No-one had realized the Soviet Union had such advanced rocket technology. Now, they had shown they were capable of building a missile powerful enough to reach North America. The Soviet R-7 rocket that fired *Sputnik* into space had been conceived from a weapon – the German V-2, the world's first long-range ballistic missile that had been developed towards the end of the

Second World War. As the Allies invaded Germany, they found the factories containing the V-2s and also the scientists working on them. Many of these scientists ended up in the United States to design the army's missiles there. Working on the Soviet rockets was chief designer Sergei Korolev, a man so important to the Soviet space programme that his identity was kept a secret. It had been Korolev who had designed the R-7 and had been responsible for the success of *Sputnik 1*. But his celebration was to be shortlived. *Sputnik 1* had been an incredible coup for the prestige of the Soviet Union, but now Soviet leader Nikita Khrushchev called for bigger and better achievements in space. The next goal was to send a man into space, and Korolev was set to work designing a capsule that could sustain life above the Earth. But they had competition. *Sputnik 1* had ignited the space race with the United States, and a frenzy of technology building and space 'firsts' followed.

The satellite *Sputnik* is launched from the Soviet Cosmodrome Baikonur, a place so secretive that it was named after a town 483km (300 miles) away to misdirect the west.

TIMELINE

1942 The first Nazi V-2 rocket is launched. Its designer, Wernher von Braun, will later work for NASA.

November 1957 Laika the dog becomes the first living creature in space.

1958 The *Explorer 1* satellite is launched by the US.

February 1959 The US launches its first spy satellite.

October 1959 The Soviet craft *Luna 2* successfully crashes onto the moon.

1942	1957	1957	1958	1958	1959	1959	1959	1960

October 1957 *Sputnik 1* becomes the first satellite in space.

January 1959 The Soviet Union launches *Luna 1*, which becomes the first man-made object to leave Earth's orbit.

1958 The National Aeronautics and Space Administration (NASA) comes into existence.

1960 An explosion at the Baikonur Cosmodrome claims the lives of 126 Soviet personnel.

FLASHPOINTS

November 1957
SPUTNIK 1

Less than a month after *Sputnik 1*, the Soviet Union became the first nation to launch a living creature into space. *Sputnik 2* was blasted into space with Laika the dog aboard. Laika was a stray who had been picked for her patience and was trained to sit still in the command seat of *Sputnik 2*. She was fitted with sensors to monitor her heart rate, nappies for her waste and oxygen tanks for air. It was never intended for Laika to survive the flight, but it later emerged that she died from heat exhaustion only six hours after lift-off. It was now clear that the Soviets would soon attempt to send a man into space.

Stray dog and *Sputnik 2* pilot Laika during space training.

December 1957
FLOPNIK

In 1957, following the successes of *Sputnik 1* and 2, the United States tried to prove it could also launch something into space. On 6 December, the press gathered for the launch of an American satellite at the Kennedy Space Center in Florida. However, shortly after lift-off, the rocket carrying the satellite exploded. The failed satellite was a bitter humiliation for the United States, and the press were quick to scathingly name it 'Flopnik'. Another attempt followed in 1958, and the United States was this time able to launch its first satellite, *Explorer 1*, into the Earth's orbit. Because *Explorer 1* was smaller than *Sputnik 1*, Soviet premier Nikita Khrushchev insultingly referred to it as 'a grapefruit'.

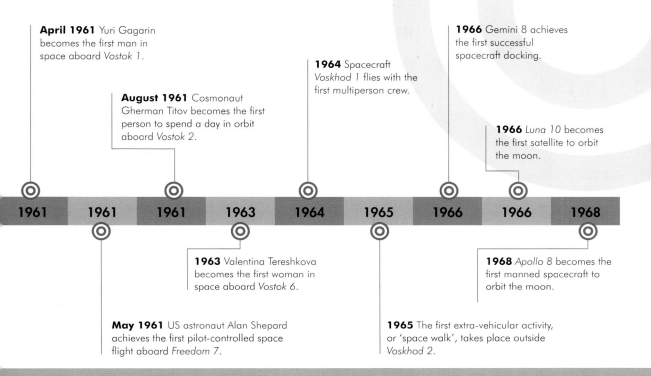

April 1961 Yuri Gagarin becomes the first man in space aboard *Vostok 1*.

August 1961 Cosmonaut Gherman Titov becomes the first person to spend a day in orbit aboard *Vostok 2*.

1964 Spacecraft *Voskhod 1* flies with the first multiperson crew.

1966 Gemini 8 achieves the first successful spacecraft docking.

1966 *Luna 10* becomes the first satellite to orbit the moon.

| 1961 | 1961 | 1961 | 1963 | 1964 | 1965 | 1966 | 1966 | 1968 |

1963 Valentina Tereshkova becomes the first woman in space aboard *Vostok 6*.

1968 *Apollo 8* becomes the first manned spacecraft to orbit the moon.

May 1961 US astronaut Alan Shepard achieves the first pilot-controlled space flight aboard *Freedom 7*.

1965 The first extra-vehicular activity, or 'space walk', takes place outside *Voskhod 2*.

1961
THE FIRST MAN IN SPACE

On 12 April, cosmonaut Yuri Gagarin became the first man in space when he was launched into the Earth's orbit aboard *Vostok 1*. Gagarin spent 108 minutes in space as *Vostok 1* travelled at 28,799kph (17,895mph) at a height of 322km (200 miles) above the Earth's surface. Gagarin re-entered the Earth's atmosphere over Siberia and parachuted to the ground over the village of Smelkovka, in Russia's Saratov region. Gagarin's landing was kept a secret for decades, as landing separately from the spacecraft would have disqualified him from the title of first man in space.

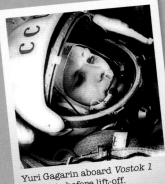

Yuri Gagarin aboard *Vostok 1* moments before lift-off.

July 1961
AMERICA REPLIES

After the success of *Vostok 1*, the United States government felt it was vital to show that it was still a player in the space race. The Mercury Seven, known as the astronauts with the 'right stuff', would be pivotal in turning NASA's space-programme dreams into reality. On 2 July 1961, Mercury Seven astronaut Alan Shepard became the first American to be launched into suborbit. Shepard's trip aboard the *Freedom 7* spacecraft was a short 15 minutes and 22 seconds, but it generated huge publicity worldwide after being broadcast live on television. America's public approach to its space programme would be in marked difference to the ultra-secretive programme of the Soviets.

1958
MAO ZEDONG INTRODUCES THE GREAT LEAP FORWARD

'To distribute resources evenly will only ruin the Great Leap Forward. When there is not enough to eat, people starve to death. It is better to let half the people die so that others can eat their fill.'

– Mao Zedong tells Communist Party of China members how he intends to make the Great Leap Forward succeed

In 1958, Communist Party chairman Mao Zedong announced plans for the new People's Republic of China to catch up with the modern nations of the world. To do this, Mao introduced a radical, countrywide overhaul known as 'The Great Leap Forward', which aimed to industrialize China as quickly as possible. With astonishing speed, China's rice fields were ploughed over, factories built and all available farmland was collectivized, meaning private ownership was abolished and was claimed by the state. Over 24,000 communes were created, each made up of around 5,000 families that controlled their own means of production. Mao believed that steel and grain would become the main pillars of the country's industrialization, and encouraged commune workers to build backyard furnaces to produce steel. Their own implements, tools and expertise were thrown into the collective commune pot, as Mao's policy did away with experts and instead forced everyone to work as equals for the common good. Mao's plan, however, was doomed from the outset and resulted in catastrophe. Workers on the communes were so preoccupied with making steel that they did not have time to produce food. Often their crops simply rotted in the fields. Meanwhile, without proper metallurgic knowledge, the steel the workers produced was mostly unusable. Regional officials, pressured to provide glowing results, wrote exaggerated reports about the grain yield. Higher party officials claimed exorbitant amounts of grain for the cities and also sold it overseas. Within months, there was not enough food and a great famine followed. It is has been estimated that up to 45 million people died from starvation, overwork, brutality and torture. While starvation wiped out 12,000 members of one commune in a few short months, other communes turned to cannibalism. Those who protested, declared their real harvest results, or simply angered officials were often beaten, tortured or buried alive. In 1962, humiliated by his failure, Mao stepped away from public view.

Chinese villagers salute their proud proletariat workers as Mao Zedong's Great Leap Forward takes root.

FLASHPOINT FACT
After Mao's death, the Communist party 'Gang of Four' received the blame for all of his wrongdoings, leaving Mao with an unblemished record.

TIMELINE

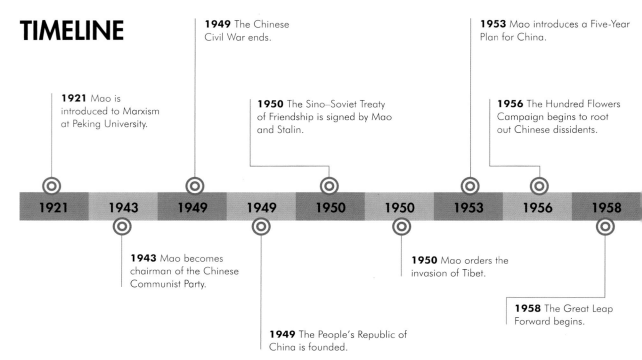

1921 Mao is introduced to Marxism at Peking University.

1949 The Chinese Civil War ends.

1950 The Sino–Soviet Treaty of Friendship is signed by Mao and Stalin.

1953 Mao introduces a Five-Year Plan for China.

1956 The Hundred Flowers Campaign begins to root out Chinese dissidents.

1921	1943	1949	1949	1950	1950	1953	1956	1958

1943 Mao becomes chairman of the Chinese Communist Party.

1950 Mao orders the invasion of Tibet.

1949 The People's Republic of China is founded.

1958 The Great Leap Forward begins.

FLASHPOINTS

1949
THE COMMUNIST RISE

Following the end of the Chinese Civil War, which was fought sporadically between 1927 and 1949, the Communist Party won control of mainland China. Their enemy, the Kuomintang (KMT) nationalist party, was left with Taiwan, Penghu, Quermoy, Matsu and several outlying islands. On 1 October 1949, Communist Party chairman Mao Zedong officially formed the People's Republic of China (PRC). China had been ravaged by war for over a century, and the PRC promised to transform it into a socialist paradise that could rival the major industrial powers of the world.

Mao Zedong sports the Chinese Communist Party uniform.

1953
THE FIVE-YEAR PLAN

The Communist Party of China began its Five-Year Plan in 1953, based partly on the Soviet model, and aimed to renew the country's economy and reshape Chinese society. The state nationalized all industry in 1955 and the country's farmers began to be organized into collectives. Any person who opposed these plans was dealt with quickly and brutally. By controlling all industry, the Communist Party controlled the economy in the same way the Soviet Union did, and ties between the two countries were initially strong. However, relations cooled as Mao opted for a more 'Chinese' model of socialism under his Great Leap Forward.

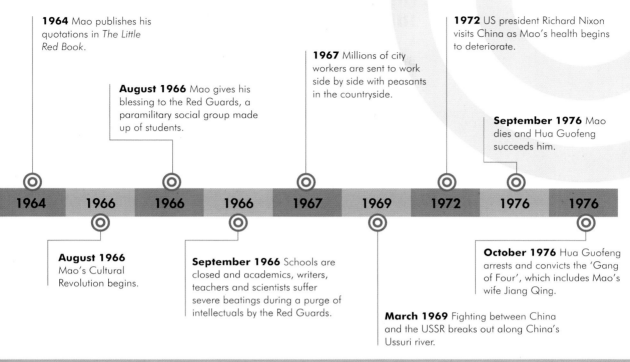

1964 Mao publishes his quotations in *The Little Red Book*.

August 1966 Mao gives his blessing to the Red Guards, a paramilitary social group made up of students.

1967 Millions of city workers are sent to work side by side with peasants in the countryside.

1972 US president Richard Nixon visits China as Mao's health begins to deteriorate.

September 1976 Mao dies and Hua Guofeng succeeds him.

1964	1966	1966	1966	1967	1969	1972	1976	1976

August 1966 Mao's Cultural Revolution begins.

September 1966 Schools are closed and academics, writers, teachers and scientists suffer severe beatings during a purge of intellectuals by the Red Guards.

March 1969 Fighting between China and the USSR breaks out along China's Ussuri river.

October 1976 Hua Guofeng arrests and convicts the 'Gang of Four', which includes Mao's wife Jiang Qing.

1960
A GREAT LEAP BACKWARDS

In 1960, Mao's Great Leap Forward was repealed after it caused several million deaths in just under two years. To try and return the country to its former levels of productivity, private plots and agricultural tools were returned to individual farmers, while other workers were allowed to work in their former areas of expertise. The system of communes was also broken up. The government introduced rationing to try and take control of the widespread starvation, but this only exacerbated the problem. Nine million people died of starvation in 1960 alone.

A Chinese worker displays the effects of the famine.

1966
CULTURAL REVOLUTION

Mao all but disappeared from public view after his disastrous Great Leap Forward, but in 1966 he returned with his 'Cultural Revolution'. Through the revolution Mao wished to purge the country of 'impure' elements, and to do so he adopted four goals: to replace the country's current leaders with those who agreed with his aims; to reform the Chinese Communist party; to give the country's youth some revolutionary experience; and to make education and other cultural systems less elitist. Mao then made himself supreme commander of the nation and sent his Red Guards to arrest intellectuals and other bourgeois elements. Over the next ten years, millions were forced into manual labour and tens of thousands were executed. Massive civil unrest followed until Mao's death in 1976, and the official end of the Cultural Revolution in 1977.

Mao's Cultural Revolution of 1966.

1960–1980

The 1960s were a time of great social and cultural change, an idealistic decade that many believed would herald a new golden era. In the west, a youth counterculture railed against war, civil-rights abuses and societal constraints. Individual choice and freedom of expression became commonplace issues, as young people 'turned on, tuned in and dropped out' to an innovative new wave of popular music. The Beatles were at the forefront of this 1960s' musical revolution, a Liverpudlian quartet that delivered a seemingly endless supply of irresistibly catchy hits for their masses of screaming fans. The Beatles were not the only popular figures to embody the 1960s' spirit of optimism and change. John F. Kennedy was America's young, charismatic president who steered the country through the Cold War Cuban Missile Crisis and promised to put an astronaut on the moon by the end of the decade. Kennedy, however, would be assassinated before this monumental space-race victory was realized. By then, the hopeful mood had waned. Student protests in Paris sparked similar demonstrations around the world, as people railed against the Vietnam War and their governments, who seemed unwilling to change. Vietnam would drag on into the mid-1970s, when a humiliated America made emergency air evacuations to escape the fall of Saigon. Fresh horrors were to follow in neighbouring Cambodia, where the Khmer Rouge instituted a ruthless programme of genocide that left millions dead. The golden age that had been hoped for by so many at the dawn of the 1960s seemed far away by the end of the 1970s.

1960

BIRTH-CONTROL PILL RELEASED TO PUBLIC

'For as long as men and women have been making babies, they've been trying not to.'

– Author Jonathan Eig, from his book *The Birth of the Pill: How Four Crusaders Reinvented Sex and Launched a Revolution*

Within five years of the birth-control pill being released to the public, 6.5 million American women were taking it. 'The Pill', as it became popularly known, created a revolution in contraception that allowed women to have control over their bodies and separate sex from pregnancy. Its 1960 release by the US Federal and Drug Administration (FDA) also coincided with the 1960s' feminist movement. After the postwar baby boom of the 1950s, many women wanted more than just motherhood and the Pill allowed them the freedom to postpone having children and pursue education and careers. Development of the Pill had been brought about by a pioneer of feminism, Margaret Sanger, and was funded by millionaire heiress Katherine McCormick. Sanger, who once ran an illegal birth-control clinic, believed that female control of contraception was simply a precondition of the emancipation of women. Women, therefore, should have a contraceptive that they were in control of. In the 1950s, Sanger approached biologist Greogry Pincus to research the possibility of using hormones for contraception. Pincus began developing a synthetic hormone that he found suppressed ovulation in animals, and soon after a gynaecologist called John Rock began testing the hormone on women. This pill, Enovid, was first approved by the FDA in 1956 for menstrual disorders such as irregular periods, but on 9 May 1960, Enovid was released as an oral contraceptive pill. The Pill was not universally applauded, however. Christian groups believed that the Pill would lead to adultery and the Pope banned its use among Catholics. Some black civil-rights leaders even criticized the Pill as being peddled to promote 'black genocide'. The Pill also attracted negative headlines in 1970 when its health risks, such as blood clots, were revealed. Safer brands were later released. Today, over 50 years after its release, more than 100 million women worldwide take the medication dubbed by *Time* magazine as 'The Pill that Unleashed Sex'.

14 December 1967: birth-control information that is shortly to be displayed on New York buses is held up for scrutiny by Marcia Goldstein, the publicity director of the Planned Parenthood organization.

TIMELINE

1725–1728AD Casanova writes about using half a lemon as a primitive cervical cap.

1870 US birth-control devices including condoms, sponges, douching syringes, diaphragms and cervical caps are made widely available from catalogues, pharmacists and dry-goods stores.

c.3000BC Condoms are made from materials such as linen sheaths, fish bladders and animal intestines.

1838 German doctor Friedrich Wilde gives patients a small cervical cap as a birth-control method.

1916 Margaret Sanger opens the first birth-control clinic in the United States.

| c. 3000BC | 23–79BC | 1725–78AC | 1832 | 1838 | 1844 | 1870 | 1873 | 1916 | 1930 |

1832 Massachusetts physician Charles Knowlton invents a birth-control solution to be syringed into the uterus after intercourse. The solution variously includes salt, vinegar, liquid chloride, zinc sulphite and aluminium potassium sulphite.

1873 The Comstock Act prohibits adverts, info and distribution of birth-control devices.

1930 Contraceptives marketed as 'feminine hygiene' products include the dangerous and ineffective Lysol douche.

23–79BC Roman writer Pliny becomes an early advocate of abstinence as a form of birth control.

1844 Charles Goodyear patents vulcanized rubber, which is then used to make rubber condoms and diaphragms.

FLASHPOINTS

1844
CONDOMS AND CRUSADES

Condoms and cervical caps, known as diaphragms, began to be manufactured in the United States after engineer Charles Goodyear patented the vulcanization of rubber in 1844. Although it took decades for diaphragms to take off, condoms caught on far more quickly. In 1861, *The New York Times* ran the first condom advertisement, for 'Dr Power's French Preventatives'. But just as contraceptives became widely available and socially acceptable, a post inspector called Anthony Comstock began a campaign against them. His moral crusade against obscenity led to the 1873 Comstock Act, which banned the spread of information about contraceptives in America.

Margaret Sanger: family-planning pioneer.

1914
REPRODUCTIVE RIGHTS

In 1914, birth-control crusader Margaret Sanger coined the phrase 'reproductive rights' in a monthly newsletter called *The Woman Rebel*. The newsletter offered its subscribers information about birth control, which contravened the country's obscenity laws. After being arrested, Sanger fled the country to avoid standing trial. Sanger later returned to the US to open the country's first family-planning clinic in 1916. The clinic was subsequently closed down by the authorities ten days later. Sanger then founded the American Birth Control League, which later became the Planned Parenthood Federation of America.

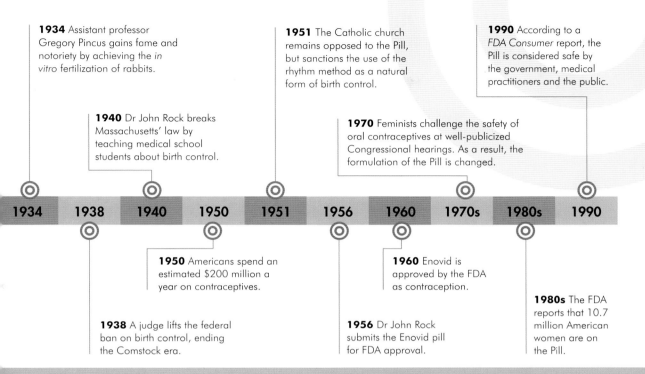

1934 Assistant professor Gregory Pincus gains fame and notoriety by achieving the *in vitro* fertilization of rabbits.

1940 Dr John Rock breaks Massachusetts' law by teaching medical school students about birth control.

1951 The Catholic church remains opposed to the Pill, but sanctions the use of the rhythm method as a natural form of birth control.

1990 According to a *FDA Consumer* report, the Pill is considered safe by the government, medical practitioners and the public.

1970 Feminists challenge the safety of oral contraceptives at well-publicized Congressional hearings. As a result, the formulation of the Pill is changed.

| 1934 | 1938 | 1940 | 1950 | 1951 | 1956 | 1960 | 1970s | 1980s | 1990 |

1950 Americans spend an estimated $200 million a year on contraceptives.

1960 Enovid is approved by the FDA as contraception.

1938 A judge lifts the federal ban on birth control, ending the Comstock era.

1956 Dr John Rock submits the Enovid pill for FDA approval.

1980s The FDA reports that 10.7 million American women are on the Pill.

1938
COMSTOCK'S COMEUPPANCE

In 1937, the American Medical Association officially recognized birth-control advice as a legitimate part of a doctor's practice. A year later, a judge lifted the federal obscenity ban on birth control, in part after a successful lawsuit filed by Sanger over the confiscation of birth-control pessaries sent from Japan. With the Comstock era now over, birth-control clinics opened across America: in 1930 there were a total of 55 clinics, and by 1942 there were over 800. Diaphragms, also known as 'womb veils', became a popular method of birth control during this time.

An early diaphragm, or 'Dutch cap'.

1950
PROVIDENTIAL MEETINGS

Millionaire philanthropist Katharine McCormick wrote to Margaret Sanger in 1950, asking her how she could fund research into developing a contraceptive pill. Later to be bankrolled by McCormick, Sanger met Gregory Pincus at a dinner party in New York and convinced him to take the research on. Unbeknown to Pincus or Sanger, a chemist called Carl Djerassi working in New Mexico had also developed a successful pill from synthesized yams, but neither he, nor his company Syntex, had any interest in testing the pill as a contraceptive. At a conference in 1952, Gregory Pincus met gynaecologist John Rock, the man who would later test Pincus's new pill on humans. Rock submitted the subsequent pill, Enovid, for FDA approval in 1956.

Enovid was the first hormonal birth-control pill, initially only given to married women.

1962
THE CUBAN MISSILE CRISIS

'If you weigh the present situation with a cool head without giving way to passion, you will understand that the Soviet Union cannot afford not to decline the despotic demands of the USA.'

– Telegram from Soviet premier Nikita Khrushchev to President John F. Kennedy, explaining why American 'piracy' in Cuban waters would lead to war

In October 1962, the United States stood on the brink of war with the Soviet Union after discovering the presence of Soviet nuclear missiles in Cuba. The trouble began in May 1960, when Soviet premier Nikita Khrushchev began delivering missiles to Cuba after promising to defend the island against hostile attack. In August, a US U-2 spy plane reported new Soviet military constructions on the island. Then, in October, spy-plane photos showed a ballistic missile standing on a launch pad. A ballistic missile launched from Cuba had the capability of hitting America within minutes, and its presence was taken as an overtly hostile act that the US could not ignore. After considering an invasion of Cuba, or airstrikes against the new missile bases, President John F. Kennedy instead ordered a military blockade or 'quarantine' around Cuba on 22 October. Kennedy then informed Khrushchev that the US would seize any offensive military material en route from Russia to Cuba. Over the next few days, Soviet ships bound for

Cuba diverted away from the quarantine zone as tension mounted on both the Soviet and US sides. As the world teetered on the brink of nuclear war, Khrushchev and Kennedy exchanged letters and telegrams. On 28 October, seven days after the crisis began, Khrushchev capitulated. He told Kennedy that the Soviet bases on Cuba would be dismantled and the missiles returned to the Soviet Union. In response, Kennedy said that the US would never invade Cuba and promised to withdraw the nuclear missiles it had been stockpiling in Turkey. As the two nations began to fulfil their promises, Cuban leader Fidel Castro raged against Khrushchev's apparent unwillingness to stand up to the Americans. Many Soviet officials felt the same way, and in October 1964, Khrushchev fell from power. However, he had succeeded in steering his country through one of the greatest crises of the 20th century: at no other time had the United States and the Soviet Union looked so close to war.

Photographs taken from a US spy plane show Soviet missile installations on the island of Cuba.

MEDIUM RANGE BALLISTIC MISSILE BASE IN CUBA

SAN CRISTOBAL

LAUNCH POSITION

MISSILE-READY TENTS

MISSILE ERECTORS

LATE OCTOBER

FLASHPOINT FACT

The Cuban Missile Crisis led to the installation of a 'hotline' between the White House and the Kremlin so that its two leaders could talk to each other directly.

TIMELINE

May 1960 The Soviet Union and Cuba establish diplomatic relations. The United States ends its foreign aid programme to Cuba.

January 1962 US intelligence reveals Soviet missile deliveries to Cuba.

January 1959 Fidel Castro assumes power after the Cuban Revolution and aligns Cuba with the Soviet Union.

January 1961 John F. Kennedy is inaugurated as the 35th president of the United States.

September 1962 Soviet foreign minister Andrei Gromyko warns America that an attack on Cuba could mean war with the Soviet Union.

1959	1959	1960	1960	1961	1961	1961	1962	1962

August 1960 The United States begins a trade embargo against Cuba.

14 October 1962 A US U-2 spy plane takes photos of Soviet missile sites on Cuba.

October 1959 Turkey and the United States agree to deploy 15 Jupiter missiles in Turkey in 1961.

April 1961 A group of Cuban exiles backed by the US invades Cuba at the Bay of Pigs, but fails to trigger an anti-Castro revolution.

FLASHPOINTS

22 October 1962
BLOCKADE ANNOUNCEMENT
On 22 October, President John F. Kennedy made a televised announcement to the American public explaining that he had ordered a blockade around Cuba and would use military force against Soviet ships entering Cuban waters. On the same day, US diplomats met with the leaders of Canada, Britain, West Germany and France to brief them on the blockade. All responded that they were supportive of the US position. In Moscow, US ambassador Foy D. Kohler briefed Khrushchev on the pending blockade. The people of the world took a deep, collective breath and waited for news. Many Americans began hoarding water, food and petrol in preparation for a nuclear war.

24 October 1962
POPE JOHN XXIII'S PLEAS
On the evening of 24 October, details of a telegram from Khrushchev to Kennedy were broadcast by Soviet news agency TASS. In the telegram, Khrushchev stated that the Soviet Union viewed the blockade as 'an act of aggression' and their ships would be instructed to ignore it. On the same day Pope John XXIII sent an imploring message to the Kremlin that said, 'We beg all governments not to remain deaf to this cry of humanity. That they do all that is in their power to save peace.' The next day the pope's message was broadcast worldwide on the radio. While having no direct impact on the negotiations, the pope's message did allow both leaders to stand back from the conflict without losing face. The message also marked the first climax of the conflict, one that enabled further discussions to be held between Washington and Moscow.

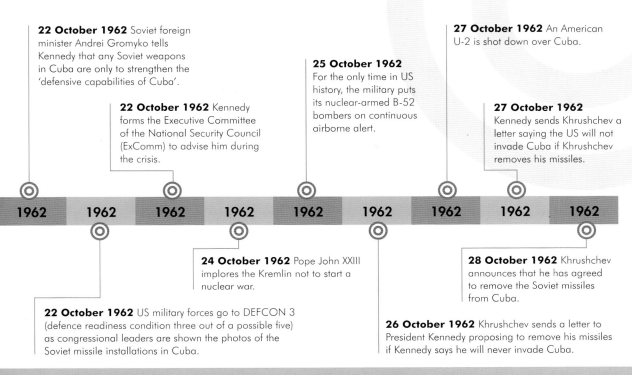

22 October 1962 Soviet foreign minister Andrei Gromyko tells Kennedy that any Soviet weapons in Cuba are only to strengthen the 'defensive capabilities of Cuba'.

22 October 1962 Kennedy forms the Executive Committee of the National Security Council (ExComm) to advise him during the crisis.

25 October 1962 For the only time in US history, the military puts its nuclear-armed B-52 bombers on continuous airborne alert.

27 October 1962 An American U-2 is shot down over Cuba.

27 October 1962 Kennedy sends Khrushchev a letter saying the US will not invade Cuba if Khrushchev removes his missiles.

| 1962 | 1962 | 1962 | 1962 | 1962 | 1962 | 1962 | 1962 | 1962 |

24 October 1962 Pope John XXIII implores the Kremlin not to start a nuclear war.

28 October 1962 Khrushchev announces that he has agreed to remove the Soviet missiles from Cuba.

22 October 1962 US military forces go to DEFCON 3 (defence readiness condition three out of a possible five) as congressional leaders are shown the photos of the Soviet missile installations in Cuba.

26 October 1962 Khrushchev sends a letter to President Kennedy proposing to remove his missiles if Kennedy says he will never invade Cuba.

25 October 1962
BOMBERS AND SHIPS

As the United States military went to DEFCON 2, it sent 23 nuclear-armed B-52 bombers to points within striking distance of the Soviet Union and put 145 intercontinental ballistic missiles on ready alert. Then the world waited as the first ships approached the US blockade. After letting oil tanker the *Bucharest* through the blockade, US warships boarded the Lebanese *Marucla* to inspect its cargo and let it pass. American intelligence reported that there had been no slow-down on the building of Soviet bases on Cuba, although the Soviet Union had turned back 14 of its ships en route to Cuba.

27 October 1962
THE ROAD TO DIPLOMACY

The crisis looked certain to come to a head after a US spy plane was shot down over Cuba on 27 October. Believing that the surface-to-air missile must have been launched by the Soviets, the US readied a Cuban invasion force in Florida. But then, on the brink of attack, Kennedy changed his mind and decided to give the Soviets the benefit of the doubt. It was later learned that Khrushchev had ordered no Soviet missiles be fired against US aircraft, as he assumed this would escalate the conflict into war. From that moment on, a way out of the crisis would be found through diplomacy.

Fidel Castro with Soviet premier Nikita Khrushchev.

US warships during their blockade of Cuba.

Profile

JOHN F. KENNEDY

John F. Kennedy was a popular president who seemed to imbue the 1960s spirit.

'My fellow Americans, ask not what your country can do for you, ask what you can do for your country.'

– John F. Kennedy makes his inauguration address in 1961, the shortest in US history at 13 minutes and 42 seconds long

At 12.30pm on 22 November 1963, shots rang out in downtown Dallas. The bullets struck American president John F. Kennedy in the neck and head as he travelled to a speaking engagement in an open-top limousine. He was pronounced dead shortly after arriving at a nearby hospital. Kennedy's assassination stunned the United States. A dynamic and popular president, Kennedy had presided over Cold War tensions with the Soviet Union and introduced groundbreaking domestic reforms, such as the expansion of civil rights to black Americans. Kennedy's ascent to power, however, had not been easy. Born into a wealthy Irish–American family, Kennedy entered politics after returning from the Second World War a naval war hero. Bankrolled by his ex-ambassador father Joseph, Kennedy was elected to the US House of Representatives in 1946 and then the Senate in 1952. Although he kept a charming and energetic

demeanour in public, behind the scenes Kennedy was plagued with health issues, including back problems and Addison's disease, which left him in constant pain. Despite taking steroids and amphetamines for pain relief, Kennedy won the Democrat party's presidential nomination in 1960 and defeated Richard Nixon in the election that same year. Kennedy's campaign had introduced America to an entirely new form of presidential politics, one based around the cult of personality rather than a figurehead toeing the party line. Kennedy was also America's youngest president at 43 years old and its first Roman Catholic. Many expected Kennedy to falter during the Cuban Missile Crisis, which occurred only two years into his presidency, but Kennedy saw off the crisis and his critics by averting war through diplomacy. He then announced that the US would defeat the Soviets in the space race by being the first nation to put a man on the moon. This would take place by Kennedy's own deadline of 1969, six years after his assassination.

US President John F. Kennedy speaks to crowds in the main auditorium of the Freie Universität, Berlin, in 1963.

FLASHPOINT FACT

Kennedy had several well-known affairs during his marriage to Jacqueline Bouvier, including one with movie star Marilyn Monroe.

TIMELINE

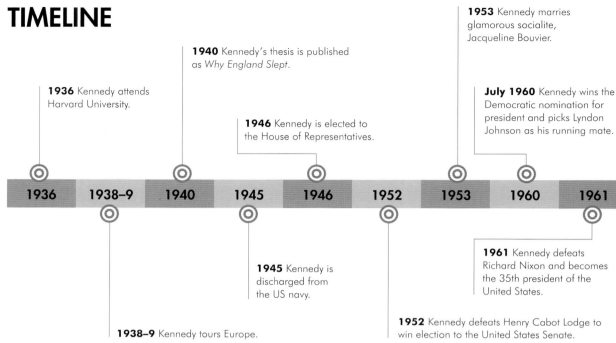

1936 Kennedy attends Harvard University.

1940 Kennedy's thesis is published as *Why England Slept*.

1946 Kennedy is elected to the House of Representatives.

1953 Kennedy marries glamorous socialite, Jacqueline Bouvier.

July 1960 Kennedy wins the Democratic nomination for president and picks Lyndon Johnson as his running mate.

| 1936 | 1938–9 | 1940 | 1945 | 1946 | 1952 | 1953 | 1960 | 1961 |

1945 Kennedy is discharged from the US navy.

1961 Kennedy defeats Richard Nixon and becomes the 35th president of the United States.

1952 Kennedy defeats Henry Cabot Lodge to win election to the United States Senate.

1938–9 Kennedy tours Europe.

FLASHPOINTS

1943
WAR HERO

After failing his military medical, Kennedy asked his father Joseph to pull some political strings to enable him to join the navy in 1941. After attending an officers' training course, Kennedy was given command of a patrol boat in 1942 and stationed in the south Pacific. In 1943, while on night patrol near the Solomon Islands, Kennedy's PT 109 boat collided with a Japanese destroyer. Two of Kennedy's men were killed instantly, but he managed to lead the remaining members through the sea to a nearby island. He then returned to the wreck to save a last, badly burned man. These brave actions won Kennedy the Navy and Marine Corps Medal and made him a war hero back in the United States.

1960
LIMELIGHT CHARMER

While on the presidential campaign trail in 1960, Kennedy faced questions on a range of tough issues that included the stalled US economy, Castro's alliance with the USSR, whether the Americans were losing the space race and Kennedy's own Roman Catholicism. By the time Kennedy participated with Republican candidate Richard Nixon in the first-ever televised presidential debate, the two candidates were neck and neck. However, television was where Kennedy came into his own. During the debate, the young and charismatic Kennedy appeared calm and confident compared to Nixon, who was visibly sweating and uncomfortable under the glare of the lights and cameras. The debate helped tip the election Kennedy's way and gave birth to a new media-savvy brand of politics that was later emulated by future presidents Bill Clinton and Barack Obama.

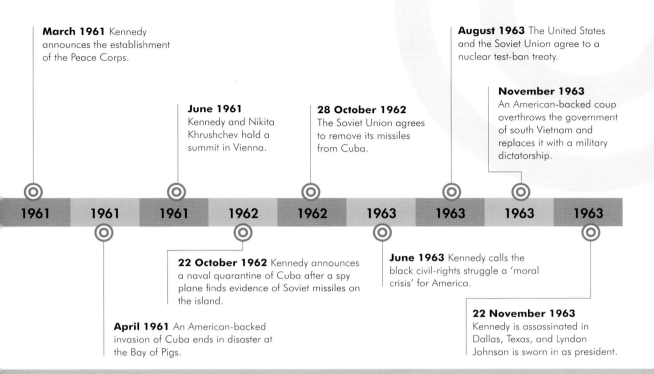

March 1961 Kennedy announces the establishment of the Peace Corps.

June 1961 Kennedy and Nikita Khrushchev hold a summit in Vienna.

28 October 1962 The Soviet Union agrees to remove its missiles from Cuba.

August 1963 The United States and the Soviet Union agree to a nuclear test-ban treaty.

November 1963 An American-backed coup overthrows the government of south Vietnam and replaces it with a military dictatorship.

1961	1961	1961	1962	1962	1963	1963	1963	1963

22 October 1962 Kennedy announces a naval quarantine of Cuba after a spy plane finds evidence of Soviet missiles on the island.

April 1961 An American-backed invasion of Cuba ends in disaster at the Bay of Pigs.

June 1963 Kennedy calls the black civil-rights struggle a 'moral crisis' for America.

22 November 1963 Kennedy is assassinated in Dallas, Texas, and Lyndon Johnson is sworn in as president.

1961
PIG OF A JOB

Only three months after his inauguration, Kennedy suffered embarrassment at home and abroad after 1,500 CIA-trained Cuban exiles failed in their attempt to invade Cuba on 17 April 1961. Approved by Kennedy, the Cuban invasion was quickly thwarted by the country's army and failed in its aims to mount an island-wide insurrection against its communist leader, Fidel Castro. Kennedy was able to re-establish his foreign-policy credibility during the Cuban Missile Crisis at the end of 1962. The young president showed his willingness to use military power against his adversary Nikita Khrushchev by blocking the delivery of Soviet missiles to Cuba, and then used diplomatic avenues to avert a nuclear war.

22 November 1963: Kennedy's assassination.

1963
ASSASSINATION

Kennedy was at the height of his popularity when he was assassinated in 1963. The route Kennedy's motorcade took on its journey through Dallas had been publicized so well-wishers could gather to welcome the president. As the procession passed the Texas School Book Depository, a lone gunman, Lee Harvey Oswald, fired three lethal shots into the president's car. Oswald was found hiding in a theatre 80 minutes later and was duly arrested, but was himself shot and killed by Jack Ruby the next day while in police custody. Ruby then died of pneumonia in 1966 while awaiting trial. The motives of both men, and the many conspiracy theories that surround Kennedy's death, continue to the present day.

Kennedy assassin Lee Harvey Oswald shortly after his arrest in November 1963.

1963

THE BEATLES RELEASE *PLEASE PLEASE ME*

'We sang it and George Martin said,
"Can we change the tempo?" We said, "What's that?"
He said, "Make it a bit faster. Let me try it."
And he did. We thought, "Oh, that's all right, yes."'

– Paul McCartney describes the making of *Please Please Me*

After having some moderate success with *Love Me Do*, the Beatles kept their fingers crossed for the release of their next single, *Please Please Me*. However, no-one could have predicted what came next. *Please Please Me* turned out to be the groundbreaker that catapulted the Beatles to fame: it brought about the phenomenon called 'Beatlemania', kicked off the 'British Invasion' of America and introduced the world to the swinging sixties. After *Please Please Me* went to number one in the UK charts, Beatles' producer George Martin was quick to get the band into the studio to cut their first album. Also called *Please Please Me*, the album was recorded in one 13-hour session, cost £400 to make and included eight original numbers from its 14-song playlist. A band playing so many of its own songs was a game-changer at a time when the charts were dominated by film soundtracks and easy-listening singers who had their music written for them. The

Beatles created a musical revolution for the throngs of screaming fans at the forefront of Beatlemania, but the band were far from newcomers to the scene. Cutting their teeth on Hamburg's 'beat music' nightclubs and then taking up a residence at The Cavern Club in Liverpool, the Beatles were already a tight live band by the time their songs hit the charts. However, it was only through the pairing of producer George Martin and manager Brian Epstein that the 'Fab Four' hit superstardom. Epstein told the band to drop their 'teddy boy' image of leather jackets and coiffed hair and replace it with smart suits and moptop haircuts. This new, improved image, combined with the catchy musical style expertly recorded by master producer George Martin, was a formula that couldn't fail. The listening public could not get enough of *Please Please Me*: it stayed at number one for 30 weeks and was only replaced by the band's second album, *With the Beatles*.

The Beatles won the hearts of the world with their charm, clean-cut image and catchy pop songs.

FLASHPOINT FACT

The album *Please Please Me* was nearly recorded before a live audience at The Cavern Club in Liverpool. However, time pressures meant that EMI booked a studio instead.

TIMELINE

August 1960 The Silver Beetles change their name to the Beatles and play at the Indra Club in Hamburg for the first time.

January 1963 *Please Please Me* reaches number one in four of the five British singles charts. Twelve number-one hits follow.

1957 John Lennon and Paul McCartney's band The Quarrymen perform at The Cavern Club in Liverpool for the first time.

June 1962 The Beatles begin their first recording session at EMI with George Martin as producer.

February 1964 The Beatles tour America for the first time and break television-viewing records on the Ed Sullivan Show.

1957	1960	1960	1960	1962	1962	1963	1963	1964	1964

1960 The Quarrymen change their name to the Silver Beetles.

October 1962 The Beatles first single, Love Me Do, reaches number 17 in the charts.

July 1964 The Beatles' debut film, *A Hard Day's Night*, premieres.

December 1960 The band play their first British concert as the Beatles at the Casbah Coffee Club in Liverpool.

November 1963 *With the Beatles* becomes the first million-selling album in Britain.

FLASHPOINTS

1957
THE QUARRYMEN

In 1957, 16-year-old John Lennon formed a skiffle group called the Quarrymen with some friends from Liverpool's Quarry Bank school. Soon afterwards, 15-year-old Paul McCartney joined as guitarist, followed by 14-year-old George Harrison. After adding drummer Pete Best, the band played 'beat music' sets in small nightclubs around Liverpool. In 1960 they moved to Hamburg, Germany, where they often played for several hours at a time in late-night drinking clubs frequented by sailors on shore leave. In late 1961, they moved back to Liverpool to take a regular spot at The Cavern Club.

The Beatles perform in Liverpool's Cavern Club, with Pete Best on drums, in 1962.

1961
MAKING MUSIC

In 1961, a Liverpool record-store owner called Brian Epstein saw the Beatles perform at The Cavern Club and immediately asked the band to let him manage them. Epstein then sent British music labels the band's tape in the hope that someone would sign them. Epstein eventually managed to secure a deal with Parlophone, a subsidiary of EMI. The producer at Parlophone who took the Beatles under his wing was the classically trained musician, George Martin. Martin suggested they replace drummer Pete Best with the more professional Ringo Starr and rearrange *Please Please Me* from a slow lament into an uplifting pop romp. History was made.

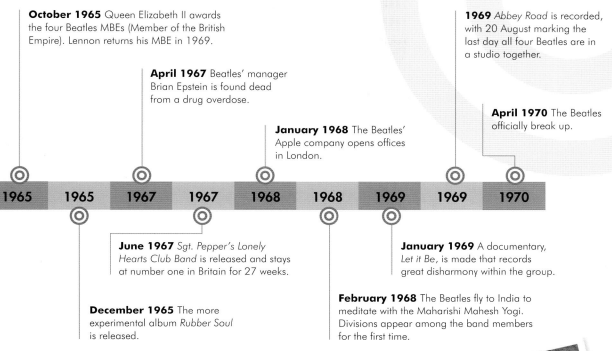

October 1965 Queen Elizabeth II awards the four Beatles MBEs (Member of the British Empire). Lennon returns his MBE in 1969.

April 1967 Beatles' manager Brian Epstein is found dead from a drug overdose.

January 1968 The Beatles' Apple company opens offices in London.

1969 *Abbey Road* is recorded, with 20 August marking the last day all four Beatles are in a studio together.

April 1970 The Beatles officially break up.

1965	1965	1967	1967	1968	1968	1969	1969	1970

June 1967 *Sgt. Pepper's Lonely Hearts Club Band* is released and stays at number one in Britain for 27 weeks.

December 1965 The more experimental album *Rubber Soul* is released.

January 1969 A documentary, *Let it Be*, is made that records great disharmony within the group.

February 1968 The Beatles fly to India to meditate with the Maharishi Mahesh Yogi. Divisions appear among the band members for the first time.

1967
SGT. PEPPER
After Beatlemania had gripped pop fans on both sides of the Atlantic – provoking the so-called British Invasion and dozens of moptop imitators – the Beatles announced their retirement from playing live. Instead, the band concentrated their efforts on recording and set to work developing an entirely different record to follow up the success of their 1966 *Revolver*. The result was the iconic 1967 *Sgt. Pepper's Lonely Hearts Club Band*, a revolutionary record that became the soundtrack for a new counterculture era of hedonism and uninhibited experimentation. Mind-expanding drugs, pacifism, free love and transcendental meditation were some of the themes that followed, as the hippie movement reached full bloom in the late 1960s.

1970
LET IT BE
In the late 1960s, personal disagreements began to break out among the Beatles' members, particularly between Paul McCartney and John Lennon, the band's leading songwriters. The Beatles had attempted to create their own company, Apple, but this had been badly mismanaged and the hard realities of financial management put a further stress on already-strained relationships. After their last studio album, *Abbey Road*, the Beatles split up in 1970. They later released *Let It Be*, an album of leftover songs. In the following years, all of the Beatles produced solo albums: John Lennon with his wife Yoko Ono and Paul McCartney with his wife Linda in his new outfit Wings. John Lennon was assassinated by a gunman in 1980, forever quashing the possibility of a Beatles reunion.

1960s London at the height of Beatlemania.

8 December 1980: John Lennon is assassinated in New York.

1965

THE US ENTERS THE VIETNAM WAR

'Well, if they say I inherited it, I'd be lucky, but they'll all say I created it…a man can fight if he can see daylight down the road somewhere, but there ain't no daylight in Vietnam. There's not a bit.'

– In a secretly taped conservation with a senator, President Lyndon B. Johnson admits he does not have control of the Vietnam War. He later announced he would not stand for re-election

America's involvement in the war between south and north Vietnam began in the 1950s. By supplying financial support and military aid to the democratic government of the south, the United States hoped to prevent the fall of the country to the communist north. To America, the Soviet and Chinese backing of the north Vietnamese guerrilla group, the Viet Cong, was a prime example of broader communist plans to subvert emerging new nations. US president John F. Kennedy felt it was up to America to provide a 'counterinsurgency' in Vietnam and prevent a domino effect of communism across southeast Asia. The incident that gave the US cause to escalate its involvement in Vietnam occurred on 2 August 1964, when north Vietnamese torpedo boats attacked the destroyer USS *Maddox* in the Gulf of Tonkin. Two days later, the United States claimed that its warship, the *Turner Joy*, had also been fired on. There was now pressure on recently elected president Lyndon Johnson to take a hard line against Ho Chi Minh's north Vietnamese government. Johnson responded by ordering retaliatory air strikes against north Vietnamese naval bases and then pushed the Gulf of Tonkin Resolution through Congress. The resolution was significant: it authorized the president to take whatever action he deemed necessary to protect US forces or its allies in southeast Asia. Johnson immediately instigated the rapid escalation of military forces in south Vietnam and subsequent open warfare with the north. In 1965, against predictions that the south was about to fall to the Viet Cong, Johnson ordered the dispatch of US troops to defend US air-force bases and wipe out Viet Cong forces in the south. In late 1965, Johnson responded to calls for a larger US force on the ground by dispatching 100,000 troops, followed by a further 100,000 in 1966. The US was now involved in full-scale war in Vietnam.

With an average age of 19, the typical soldier in Vietnam was exposed to a brutal form of jungle warfare that the United States could not win.

FLASHPOINT FACT

In 1971, *The New York Times* published a leaked document known as the Pentagon Papers, which showed that four successive presidents had lied to the American public about their intentions in Vietnam. Among other things, the document showed that the military was secretly bombing parts of Laos and Cambodia.

TIMELINE

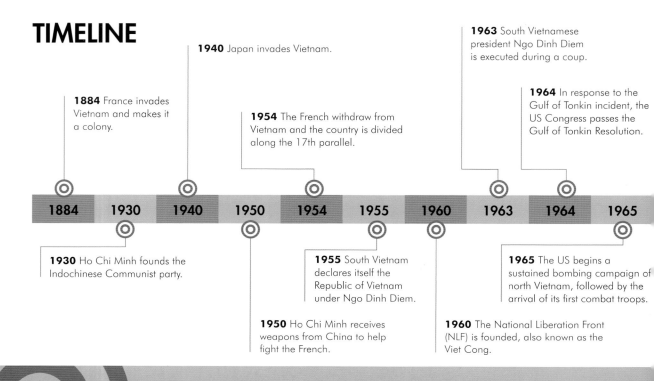

1884 France invades Vietnam and makes it a colony.

1940 Japan invades Vietnam.

1954 The French withdraw from Vietnam and the country is divided along the 17th parallel.

1963 South Vietnamese president Ngo Dinh Diem is executed during a coup.

1964 In response to the Gulf of Tonkin incident, the US Congress passes the Gulf of Tonkin Resolution.

| 1884 | 1930 | 1940 | 1950 | 1954 | 1955 | 1960 | 1963 | 1964 | 1965 |

1930 Ho Chi Minh founds the Indochinese Communist party.

1950 Ho Chi Minh receives weapons from China to help fight the French.

1955 South Vietnam declares itself the Republic of Vietnam under Ngo Dinh Diem.

1960 The National Liberation Front (NLF) is founded, also known as the Viet Cong.

1965 The US begins a sustained bombing campaign of north Vietnam, followed by the arrival of its first combat troops.

FLASHPOINTS

1959
DESPOT DIEM

With support from the US military, Ngo Dinh Diem installed himself as leader of south Vietnam, called the Republic of Vietnam, in 1955. However, Diem's dictatorial and discriminatory polices led to protests, infighting and weakening of his government's credibility. In 1957, many disaffected non-communist south Vietnamese joined the ranks of the north's communist Viet Cong, which had begun assassinations and acts of terrorism against Diem's government. By 1959, these largely guerrilla actions had developed into open firefights between the south Vietnamese army, known as the ARVN, and the Viet Cong, which was supported by Ho Chi Minh in the north. War had begun.

1965
TERROR FROM THE SKIES

To support its ground troops in Vietnam, the US military began constructing logistical infrastructure in 1965, including 75 new airbases. From here, the US unleashed the full strength of its air force onto the Viet Cong and the north Vietnamese army (NVA), including air strikes, armed helicopter attacks and B-52 bombing raids. The intention was to decimate the enemy from the air and then send in US troops to pick off the pockets of enemy resistance left alive. By bombing strongholds in the jungle, the Americans hoped to destroy the enemy's supply lines and fresh soldiers preparing to join the front line. But the Viet Cong and NVA were not destroyed as the US military hoped, and became adept at hiding and then reoccupying areas once the Americans had passed through.

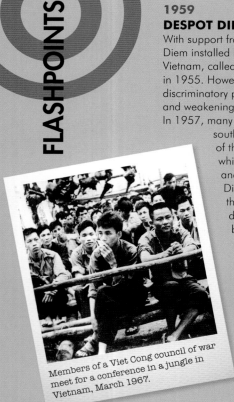

Members of a Viet Cong council of war meet for a conference in a jungle in Vietnam, March 1967.

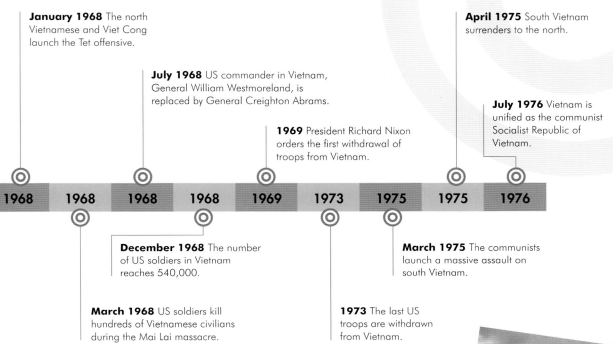

January 1968 The north Vietnamese and Viet Cong launch the Tet offensive.

April 1975 South Vietnam surrenders to the north.

July 1968 US commander in Vietnam, General William Westmoreland, is replaced by General Creighton Abrams.

July 1976 Vietnam is unified as the communist Socialist Republic of Vietnam.

1969 President Richard Nixon orders the first withdrawal of troops from Vietnam.

| 1968 | 1968 | 1968 | 1968 | 1969 | 1973 | 1975 | 1975 | 1976 |

December 1968 The number of US soldiers in Vietnam reaches 540,000.

March 1975 The communists launch a massive assault on south Vietnam.

March 1968 US soldiers kill hundreds of Vietnamese civilians during the Mai Lai massacre.

1973 The last US troops are withdrawn from Vietnam.

1968
TET OFFENSIVE

As the war in Vietnam became increasingly unpopular in America, the communists plotted a bold stoke against the south that they hoped would end its resistance and convince the Americans to go home. The action began in January 1968, as the NVA and Viet Cong began a series of diversionary attacks on targets such as the US marine base at Khe Sanh, northwest Vietnam. Then, as US and south Vietnamese troops were occupied defending their bases, the communists launched their lunar new year or 'Tet' offensive in south Vietnam, attacking five of its six cities and 36 of its 44 provincial capitals. Despite only occupying the invaded areas for one or two days, the communists' Tet offensive had done the damage in Washington. The US government began plans to wind up its involvement in the war soon afterwards.

1975
FALL OF SAIGON

In 1973, the US admitted its failure in the Vietnam War and gave in to the demands of protestors at home by suing for peace. Although Vietnamese soldiers kept fighting, America stopped its eight-year bombing campaign of the country and began to withdraw its military in large numbers. Meanwhile, the communists launched 'Campaign 275', which decimated the ARVN forces in the country's strategic central highlands. As the ARVN retreated, the NVA marched towards the south Vietnamese capital Saigon and surrounded the city. As the city fell, the last Americans made a hasty evacuation by helicopter. With the fall of Saigon, the Vietnam War was over.

American UH1 Huey.

1968
THE PARIS STUDENT PROTESTS

'I greet the year 1968 with serenity. It is impossible to see how France today could be paralyzed by crisis as she has been in the past.'

– French President Charles de Gaulle broadcasts his annual new year message to the nation

In the spring of 1968, Paris stunned the world with student and worker protests that nearly brought the country to its knees. The unrest began at the Sorbonne University's Nanterre campus, where students had been voicing their dissatisfaction for months over their underfunded education system. On 2 May the police shut down the university, which led to several days of marches, demonstrations and riots. The worst of the violence occurred on 6 May, as police fired teargas and charged at crowds of over 20,000 marching students and university teachers with their batons raised. After several hours of clashes between protestors and the police, the city's cultural centre, St Germain des Prés, resembled a battlefield. Shop windows were smashed, bus tyres slashed and cars overturned, as Red Cross workers in helmets ducked under clouds of teargas to give first aid to hundreds of casualties. Television images of students covered with blood were broadcast to shocked audiences around the world, as

police clubbed protestors armed with stones and torn-up pieces of tarmac. More riots followed on 10 May, as worker and student unions called for a nationwide strike against 'police repression' and demanded the release of all arrested protestors. On 13 May, over one million students and striking workers marched through the streets of Paris. The government tried to placate the protestors by announcing the release of the prisoners and the reopening of the Sorbonne. However, this did not prevent further protests, which culminated in the burning of the Paris stock exchange, President Charles de Gaulle fleeing the country and a nationwide strike of millions of French workers. In the end, however, the revolution did not come, although the Paris protests are considered a moral and cultural turning point in the country's modern history. They also inspired similar actions around the world, as students and workers demonstrated against the Vietnam War and their own authoritarian governments.

Students riding on top of cars and waving flags at night during the pro-de Gaulle demonstration march down the Champs-Élysées in Paris, 1968.

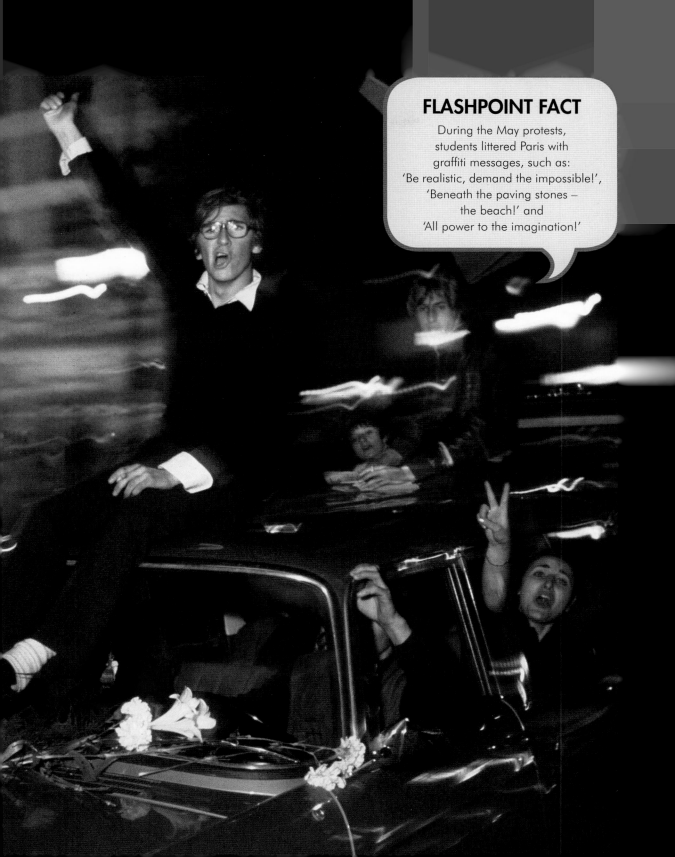

FLASHPOINT FACT

During the May protests, students littered Paris with graffiti messages, such as: 'Be realistic, demand the impossible!', 'Beneath the paving stones – the beach!' and 'All power to the imagination!'

TIMELINE

8 March 1968 A Polish political crisis begins after University of Warsaw students are beaten with clubs during a march for student rights.

16 March 1968 An anti-Vietnam War protest outside the US embassy in Grosvenor Square, London, leads to hours of street fighting between police and demonstrators.

22 March 1968 Students invade the Sorbonne University's Nanterre administration building.

6 May 1968 Paris student protests erupt into five hours of rioting with police.

7 May 1968 A 50,000-strong march against police brutality turns into further violent clashes in Paris's Latin Quarter.

| 1968 | 1968 | 1968 | 1968 | 1968 | 1968 | 1968 | 1968 | 1968 |

April 1968 American students occupy Columbia University, forcing it to close.

16 March 1968 Over 400 University of Rome students are arrested after protesting against Italian police brutality.

2 May 1968 The Sorbonne University is closed down by French authorities.

10 May 1968 Another huge crowd congregates on Paris's Left Bank. Occupations and demonstrations soon spread throughout France.

FLASHPOINTS

22 March 1968
SORBONNE SHUTS

After protests at the Sorbonne's Nanterre campus erupted in March, the police arrested four of its students, the first of many over the following months. On this occasion, the students had been staging an anti-Vietnam War rally, although many other protests were also held. Often the students demonstrated against substandard conditions on campus, as well as an education system they believed was outdated and inadequately funded. After the arrests several hundred students, who later formed the *Mouvement du 22 Mars* ('Movement of 22 March'), stormed the university buildings. This action, in part, led to the police closure of the Sorbonne on 2 May.

May 1968 – injured students help each other in the aftermath of a demonstration in Paris.

10 May 1968
SYMPATHY STRIKES

After the riots of 6 May, a huge crowd congregated on Paris's Left Bank on 10 May. After the police blocked the protestors from crossing the river, clashes once again broke out as the crowd knocked over the barricades that had been erected to contain them. The street riots lasted until dawn the next day and the injuries and arrests were once again broadcast on television to viewers around the world. Many of the protestors alleged *agents provocateurs* had been employed by the government to throw Molotov cocktails and burn cars. The police brutality that occurred during the demonstration brought sympathy from many French worker unions, which called for a one-day general strike on 13 May.

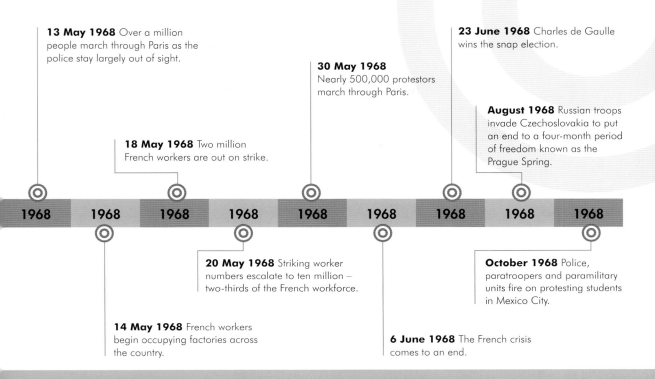

13 May 1968 Over a million people march through Paris as the police stay largely out of sight.

18 May 1968 Two million French workers are out on strike.

30 May 1968 Nearly 500,000 protestors march through Paris.

23 June 1968 Charles de Gaulle wins the snap election.

August 1968 Russian troops invade Czechoslovakia to put an end to a four-month period of freedom known as the Prague Spring.

| 1968 | 1968 | 1968 | 1968 | 1968 | 1968 | 1968 | 1968 | 1968 |

20 May 1968 Striking worker numbers escalate to ten million – two-thirds of the French workforce.

October 1968 Police, paratroopers and paramilitary units fire on protesting students in Mexico City.

14 May 1968 French workers begin occupying factories across the country.

6 June 1968 The French crisis comes to an end.

20 May 1968
FRANCE STOPS

During the week beginning 20 May, over ten million French workers went out on strike. Inspired by the student protests, the workers used the civil unrest as an opportunity to demand higher wages, better working conditions and the ousting of Charles de Gaulle as French president. De Gaulle responded by saying that France faced civil war and was 'on the brink of paralysis'. His words were followed by several hundred protesting students storming the Paris stock exchange and setting it alight. Within hours, the fire in the stock exchange had been put out and it emerged that de Gaulle had fled the country for Germany.

23 June 1968
COMEBACK DE GAULLE

As the French government seemed close to collapse, Charles de Gaulle considered standing down. But after being assured that he still had control of the military, if not the country, de Gaulle decided to try and stay in power. Although the national television service was on strike, de Gaulle made an announcement on French radio that he would dissolve the country's national assembly so a snap election could take place on 23 June.

He also ordered all striking workers to return to work or he would institute a state of emergency. In the end, most strikers did return to work and the students called off their street demonstrations. As the movement lost its momentum many people came out in support of de Gaulle, who subsequently won the election on 23 June.

Workers join the strike.

1969

NEIL ARMSTRONG BECOMES THE FIRST MAN ON THE MOON

The *Apollo 11* astronauts: Neil Armstrong, Michael Collins and Buzz Aldrin.

'Here men from the planet Earth first set foot upon the moon July 1969AD. We came in peace for all mankind.'

– A plaque left on the *Apollo 11* lunar module Eagle, the craft that safely transported the first men on to the moon

A s Neil Armstrong slowly climbed down the ladder of the *Eagle* lunar module, he was not exactly sure what lay below. Thousands of scientists, designers and engineers at NASA had sent three men 386,400km (240,000 miles) from Earth to explore a new world for the first time – but nobody could predict what its surface would be like. As millions of TV viewers on Earth held their breath, Armstrong lowered a tentative foot to the ground and then stepped safely onto the lunar soil. Then, there was a collective sigh of relief and joy as Armstrong uttered his immortal words: 'That's one small step for men, one giant leap for mankind.' The moon landing symbolized America's victory over the Soviet Union in the space race, which had begun over a decade earlier. At that time the race belonged to the Soviets, who seemed to make one space breakthrough after another. Determined not

to be outdone, President John F. Kennedy made the extraordinary claim that America would have a man on the moon by the end of the decade. The experts at NASA did a double-take at this announcement. America had only just launched a man into suborbit and even its top scientists hadn't conceived of a rocket that could fly as far as the moon. However, in 1969 NASA seemed to have fulfilled Kennedy's wish when *Apollo 11* blasted its way out of Earth's orbit and towards the moon. But it was not until Armstrong set foot on to the lunar surface that the success of the moon mission was assured. The astronauts left their footprints in the fine, powdery soil for posterity, but some of it found its way back to Earth, as Armstrong explained during his first phone call back on Earth: 'Hello, Mom, this is Neil…it was fantastically beautiful. The surface is covered with a black dust, and it got all over our nice, clean, white suits and wouldn't brush off.'

Buzz Aldrin salutes the Stars and Stripes, a flag specially constructed to look as though it were flapping in the wind.

FLASHPOINT FACT

The total computing power of *Apollo 11*'s command module was less than that of a mobile phone today.

TIMELINE

May 1966 US *Surveyor 1* makes the second soft landing on the moon, a few months after Soviet probe *Luna 9*.

December 1968 Frank Borman, James Lovell and William Anders begin the first manned journey from the Earth to the moon aboard *Apollo 8*.

January 1969 *Soyuz 4* and *5* perform the first Soviet spacecraft docking.

March 1968 The first man in space, cosmonaut Yuri Gagarin, dies in a plane crash.

June 1969 Neil Armstrong and Edwin 'Buzz' Aldrin become the first men on the moon while crewmate Michael Collins orbits around it.

1966	1966	1967	1967	1968	1968	1969	1969	1970

August 1966 Unmanned US *Orbiter 1* enters orbit around the moon.

April 1967 Cosmonaut Vladimir Komarov is killed when the parachutes of his *Soyuz 1* capsule fail to open on re-entry.

January 1967 Three astronauts are killed in a fire aboard their *Apollo 1* command module.

April 1970 On its journey to the moon, *Apollo 13* suffers from an explosion and its astronauts have to carry out improvised repairs to get home safely.

FLASHPOINTS

1962
THE US CATCHES UP

In 1961, after the United States had successfully launched Alan Shepard into suborbit for 15 minutes, President Kennedy announced the most ambitious space plan ever proposed: 'This nation should commit itself to achieving the goal, before the decade is out, of landing a man on the moon and returning him safely to the Earth.' The news shocked many people at NASA, but armed with a staggering budget of $20 billion the space agency set about making Kennedy's dream a reality. The first step was to match the Soviet achievement of launching a man into orbit. This was finally accomplished on 20 February 1962, when John Glenn became the first US astronaut to orbit the Earth aboard Mercury spacecraft, *Friendship 7*. Nearly a year after *Vostok 1*, the US had finally caught up with its Soviet rival.

1966
SPACE EMERGENCY

To land a man on the moon, NASA had to be able to dock two spacecraft together in space. In March 1966, NASA's most experienced pilot Neil Armstrong was launched into space aboard *Gemini 8*, to dock with an unmanned rocket there. However, after catching up to the rocket and successfully docking with it, the two craft went into a spin. Armstrong managed to separate the spacecraft, but *Gemini 8* continued to spin out of control. The only solution was to abort the mission and fire *Gemini*'s re-entry thrusters to gain control of the craft. No-one was hurt as *Gemini 8* made an emergency splashdown into the Pacific Ocean, but the incident was a stark reminder that things could go badly wrong in space.

A scale model of the Apollo 11 command module.

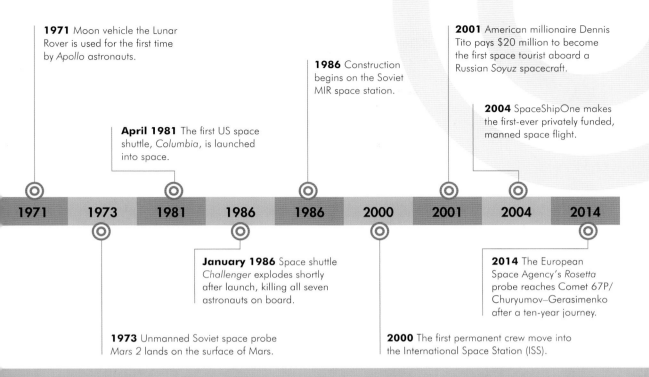

1971 Moon vehicle the Lunar Rover is used for the first time by *Apollo* astronauts.

1986 Construction begins on the Soviet MIR space station.

2001 American millionaire Dennis Tito pays $20 million to become the first space tourist aboard a Russian *Soyuz* spacecraft.

2004 SpaceShipOne makes the first-ever privately funded, manned space flight.

April 1981 The first US space shuttle, *Columbia*, is launched into space.

| 1971 | 1973 | 1981 | 1986 | 1986 | 2000 | 2001 | 2004 | 2014 |

January 1986 Space shuttle *Challenger* explodes shortly after launch, killing all seven astronauts on board.

2014 The European Space Agency's *Rosetta* probe reaches Comet 67P/Churyumov–Gerasimenko after a ten-year journey.

1973 Unmanned Soviet space probe *Mars 2* lands on the surface of Mars.

2000 The first permanent crew move into the International Space Station (ISS).

1967
APOLLO TRAGEDY

In January 1967, the United States suffered its first great space tragedy when astronauts Virgil Grissom, Ed White and Roger Chaffee were killed during testing of *Apollo 1*. *Apollo 1* was scheduled to become the first manned Apollo mission into space, and the accident took place during a routine practice run of the spacecraft's launch. The three astronauts had boarded *Apollo 1*'s command module and its hatch was bolted on behind them. Suddenly, a chilling cry came over the radio: 'We've got a fire in the cockpit!'. The flash fire that swept through the command module reached such an intense heat that all three astronauts were killed within minutes before the hatch could be removed. A report later revealed that NASA had cut corners in its race to get a man to the moon.

The burnt-out remains of *Apollo 1*.

1968
MOON MISSION SUCCESS

In reaction to fears that the Soviet Union was planning a lunar landing, the US launched its first spacecraft to the moon: *Apollo 8*. On 21 December 1968, *Apollo 8* orbited the Earth once before its rockets fired it to an 'escape velocity' of 40,234kph (25,000mph) to push it out of Earth's orbit. Less than three days later, *Apollo 8*'s rockets fired again to put it into the moon's orbit. Those at NASA held their breath as *Apollo 8* travelled around the moon to its far side – a place never seen by human eyes. Then, to everyone's relief, *Apollo 8* emerged on the other side. The astronauts on board then glimpsed something never seen before: the Earth rising above the moon's horizon, or 'Earthrise'. The United States had proved that the moon was now within its reach.

1975
CAMBODIAN GENOCIDE BEGINS UNDER POL POT

'I did not join the resistance movement to kill people, to kill the nation. Look at me now. Am I a savage person? My conscience is clear.'

– Khmer Rouge leader Pol Pot discusses his involvement in the four-year genocide in Cambodia

The Khmer Rouge was a little-known force of guerrilla fighters when it entered the capital of Cambodia as a liberating army. But few of the well-wishers welcoming the Khmer Rouge into Phnom Penh in 1975 could have predicted the horrors about to be unleashed by their new, brutal overlords. Led by Pol Pot, the communist Khmer Rouge had originally been formed to oppose French colonial rule in Cambodia. In the 1970s, the Khmer Rouge then fought against US-backed general Lon Nol in Cambodia's civil war. When the US withdrew from Vietnam, Lon Nol's regime collapsed and the Khmer Rouge seized control. From the outset, Pot made his intentions clear. His troops marched the entire two-million strong population of Phnom Penh into the countryside and forced them to work in the rice fields at gunpoint. This procedure was repeated in other cities as 'Year Zero' was instituted: an eight-point plan that Pot said would 'purify' Cambodia from capitalism and transform it into an agrarian socialist society. Money and private property were abolished as schools, hospitals, monasteries and businesses were closed down. Religion was banned, books were burned and modern machines smashed during the mass exodus of the cities. Many thousands died during the subsequent forced marches into the countryside. Pot's plan to purify Cambodian society along religious, racial, social and political lines led to ruthless nationwide purges. Leaders of industry, journalists, students, doctors, lawyers and ethnic and religious minorities were all targeted, as the Khmer Rouge began its plan to create a new Cambodian master race. The results were devastating. During its rule between 1975 and 1979, the Khmer Rouge killed an estimated two million Cambodians from forced labour, starvation, disease, torture and execution. Many were buried in mass graves known as the 'Killing Fields', and the genocide only ended when the country was invaded by Vietnam in 1979.

One of the many mounds of bones that make up the terrible legacy of the Khmer Rouge's reign.

FLASHPOINT FACT

Under the Khmer Rouge, anyone perceived as being an intellectual faced execution, including people who wore glasses. This, the regime said, showed they spent too much time reading instead of working.

TIMELINE

1863 Cambodia becomes a protectorate of France.

1953 Cambodia wins its independence from France and becomes the kingdom of Cambodia under King Sihanouk.

1969 The US military begins bombing north Vietnamese forces in Cambodia.

1975 Lon Nol is overthrown by the Khmer Rouge, led by Pol Pot. 'Year Zero' begins.

1977 Fighting breaks out between Democratic Kampuchea and Vietnam.

1863	1946	1953	1965	1969	1970	1975	1976	1977	1979

1946 France reimposes its protectorate after Japanese occupation during the Second World War ends. Communist guerrillas begin a campaign against the French.

1965 Sihanouk severs ties with the US and allows north Vietnamese soldiers to set up bases in Cambodia.

1970 General Lon Nol overthrows Sihanouk in a military coup.

1976 Cambodia is renamed Democratic Kampuchea, as Khieu Samphan becomes head of state and Pol Pot prime minister.

1979 The Vietnamese invade Democratic Kampuchea, bringing an end to the genocide.

FLASHPOINTS

1973
COLLUDING KING

In 1970, Cambodia's ruler King Sihanouk colluded with the north Vietnamese army, allowing them to operate from within Cambodia as they fought in the Vietnam War. This led to the secret US carpet-bombing of Cambodia and a subsequent US-backed coup led by Cambodian general, Lon Nol. In retaliation, Prince Sihanouk joined forces with the Khmer Rouge in 1973 to oust Lon Nol, a corrupt and tyrannical leader who only maintained control through his US support. When America withdrew from Vietnam, the Khmer Rouge overthrew Lon Nol in 1975 and Prince Sihanouk returned from exile. However, Sihanouk was put under house arrest for the duration of the Khmer Rouge's reign.

1975
GENOCIDE BEGINS

When the Khmer Rouge took power in 1975, thousands of monks were stripped of their robes and forced to tend the fields, as soldiers occupied the iconic 12th-century Cambodian temple of Angkor Wat. Hundreds of thousands of the educated middle classes were then arrested, tortured and murdered in specially made execution centres. Many ethnic groups were also victimized, particularly those from the Muslim Cham minority. It is estimated that up to 500,000 Cham people were killed under the Khmer Rouge, leaving only 200,000 survivors.

Human remains left over from Pol Pot's ethnic cleansing.

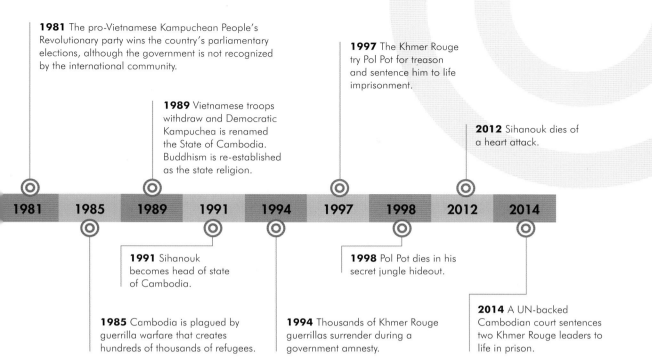

1981 The pro-Vietnamese Kampuchean People's Revolutionary party wins the country's parliamentary elections, although the government is not recognized by the international community.

1989 Vietnamese troops withdraw and Democratic Kampuchea is renamed the State of Cambodia. Buddhism is re-established as the state religion.

1997 The Khmer Rouge try Pol Pot for treason and sentence him to life imprisonment.

2012 Sihanouk dies of a heart attack.

| 1981 | 1985 | 1989 | 1991 | 1994 | 1997 | 1998 | 2012 | 2014 |

1991 Sihanouk becomes head of state of Cambodia.

1998 Pol Pot dies in his secret jungle hideout.

1985 Cambodia is plagued by guerrilla warfare that creates hundreds of thousands of refugees.

1994 Thousands of Khmer Rouge guerrillas surrender during a government amnesty.

2014 A UN-backed Cambodian court sentences two Khmer Rouge leaders to life in prison.

1979
THE KILLING FIELDS

Although the Khmer Rouge and Vietnam shared the same communist beliefs, tensions mounted between the two in the late 1970s. In 1979, Vietnam invaded Cambodia and forced the Khmer Rouge to seek refuge in the country's mountainous region along the Thai border. From here, Pol Pot staged a number of guerrilla actions against the Vietnamese rulers, although he was not able to regain power. Meanwhile, gruesome evidence of the Khmer Rouge's atrocities were uncovered – mass graves, known today as the Killing Fields.

The Cambodian Killing Fields.

2009
LEADERSHIP TRIALS

After years of running the Khmer Rouge as a guerrilla force, in 1997 the organization fell into decline. Pol Pot was ousted as leader, put under house arrest for treason by his colleagues and died in 1998. In 2001, the Cambodian government passed legislation that allowed for some of the Khmer Rouge's leadership to be tried for their crimes. The trials began in 2009. In 2014, Nuon Chea, or 'Brother Number Two', and Khmer Rouge head of state, Khieu Samphan, were convicted of crimes against humanity and sentenced to life imprisonment.

Young Khmer Rouge guerrilla soldiers.

1980–2000

The last decades of the 20th century represented the rise of globalization, as political ideologies fell and people were united by protest, information technology and the growing threat of climate change. The early 1980s opened to a climate of fear and prejudice, when the outbreak of AIDS caused many to point the finger at homosexuals, heroin users, haemophiliacs and Haitians. AIDS would hit South Africa particularly hard, a country that shook off its apartheid shroud in the 1990s and freed the founding father of its new democracy, Nelson Mandela. Mandela's release proved the power of popular resistance against an oppressive regime; it also showed the strength of international pressure in bringing about political change. But civil disobedience could bring mixed results: Chinese soldiers indiscriminately shot and killed students protesting in Tiananmen Square, while mass demonstrations in communist Europe brought about the fall of the Berlin Wall and the collapse of the Soviet Union. As those nations formerly behind the Iron Curtain became free to adopt democratic elections and capitalist economic models, developments in communications made the world a more culturally homogenized place. Globalization was the buzzword for the century's end, as the new World Wide Web linked up people around the planet. The Web also spread troubling news about climate change and the impact of damaging greenhouse gases caused by human industry. While the Industrial Revolution had enabled great technological advances to be made in the 20th century, this progress had come at a price. Climate change, the great environmental issue of the late 20th century, would be left to the people of the 21st century to resolve.

1981
THE OUTBREAK OF AIDS

*'You can't get AIDS from a hug or a handshake
or a meal with a friend.'*

– Basketball player Earvin 'Magic' Johnson tries to dispel myths and
misconceptions surrounding the spread of AIDS .

In the early 1980s
posters such as this
one were plastered
up around UK cities,
as the government
launched a public
health campaign to
tackle AIDS.

In June 1981, five homosexual men in Los Angeles were diagnosed with a rare lung infection known as *Pneumocystis carinii* pneumonia. A report into the cases by the Centers for Disease Control and Prevention (CDC) found that the disease had probably been spread through sexual contact and seemed to be linked to immune dysfunction. The following month, the CDC reported the outbreak of a rare cancer called Kaposi's sarcoma among homosexual men in San Francisco and New York. The CDC noted that sufferers of the cancer were also presenting symptoms of *Pneumocystis carinii* pneumonia, and other opportunistic infections. Researchers found that the infections and cancers were part of an acquired immunodeficiency syndrome, which they then labelled GRID (Gay-Related Immune Deficiency). By 1982, however, it became clear that the disease did not exclusively infect homosexual men: intravenous drug users were also showing symptoms. The CDC then coined the phrase

'the 4H disease', as those most commonly affected appeared to be homosexuals, heroin users, haemophiliacs and Haitians. However, as people not belonging to one of the '4H' categories were also contracting the disease, it was subsequently renamed Acquired Immune Deficiency Syndrome, or AIDS. It emerged that AIDS was the last stage of a retrovirus called human immunodeficiency virus, or HIV. HIV/AIDS became the most devastating infectious disease of the late 20th century and its outbreak created a climate of fear, panic and prejudice across modern society. Right-wing religious groups saw the disease as divine retribution against immorality, while conspiracists propagated theories on germ warfare and Cold War experiments gone wrong. A cure for AIDS has not yet been discovered, and the numbers killed by the pandemic serve as a tragic reminder of its devastating effectiveness. As of 2013, HIV/AIDS had caused over 36 million deaths worldwide and around 37 million people are currently living with the disease.

FLASHPOINT FACT

According to the World Health Organization, the rate of infection between couples where one partner is HIV-positive is less than one per cent if condoms are used.

AIDS IS NOT PREJUDICED

IT CAN KILL ANYONE.

GAY OR STRAIGHT, MALE OR FEMALE, ANYONE CAN GET AIDS FROM SEXUAL INTERCOURSE. SO THE MORE PARTNERS, THE GREATER THE RISK. PROTECT YOURSELF, USE A CONDOM.

TIMELINE

1966 HIV is first estimated to have arrived in the Americas in Haiti. The man carrying the disease was probably first infected in the Congo, Africa.

1969 St Louis teenager Robert Rayford dies from a mystery disease later found to be HIV.

1982 A Californian baby becomes the first infant to contract AIDS from a blood transfusion.

1980 San Francisco resident Ken Horne becomes the first recognized AIDS case in the US.

1983 The CDC National AIDS Hotline is set up.

| 1966 | 1968 | 1969 | 1979 | 1980 | 1982 | 1982 | 1983 | 1984 |

1979 The first known American baby to be born with AIDS dies.

1982 The CDC reports a cluster of opportunistic infections and Kaposi's sarcoma among Haitians entering the United States.

1984 Scientist Robert Gallo discovers the probable cause of AIDS is the retrovirus human immunodeficiency virus, or HIV.

1968 HIV arrives in the United States.

FLASHPOINTS

1930s
AIDS ORIGINS

Although its exact origins remain unclear, researchers believe HIV/AIDS was spread to humans via primates from west-central Africa. The two strains of HIV, HIV-1 and HIV-2, probably originated from Old World monkeys, such as chimpanzees in Cameroon and sooty mangabeys from coastal west Africa. These primates are thought to have been carrying strains of simian immunodeficiency virus (SIV), which in turn evolved into HIV-1 and HIV-2 in humans. It is thought that SIV was passed to humans through the butchering and eating of primate meat in the 1930s. The rise of colonialism then allowed the disease to pass through high-transmission areas such as ports, where sexual promiscuity and prostitution were common.

1959
THE FIRST CASE OF HIV

The world's first known case of AIDS in a human is thought to have occurred in the Democratic Republic of Congo in 1959. A preserved sample of the dead man's blood was investigated in the 1990s and genes connected with HIV were discovered. In the same year, Ardouin Antonio, a New York shipping clerk, died of the *Pneumocystis carinii* pneumonia so prevalent among the Los Angeles AIDS cases of 1981. The postmortem doctor found the infection in Antonio's lungs so unusual that he preserved them for future study, and later said that the man had died from AIDS.

An AIDS scientist takes blood from a primate.

1984 Haemophiliac Ryan White is barred from his school after being infected with HIV from a blood transfusion.

1986 US lawyer Geoffrey Bowers is fired from his law firm for having AIDS, which later inspired the film *Philadelphia*, starring Tom Hanks.

1998 The Treatment Action Campaign is launched to campaign for greater HIV treatment access for South Africans.

2005 The CDC recommends anti-retroviral post-exposure prophylaxis (PEP) to be taken for a month by those exposed to HIV through rape, accident, unsafe sex or drug use.

2013 According to a French study, 12 out of 75 people who take combination antiretroviral therapy become 'functionally cured' of HIV.

1984	1985	1986	1996	1998	2000	2005	2013	2015

1996 Scientist Robert Gallo discovers natural compounds called chemokines can block HIV and halt the progression of AIDS.

2000 The World Health Organization estimates that between 15 and 20 per cent of new HIV cases are from transfusions of inadequately screened blood.

1985 American actor Rock Hudson dies of AIDS. Hudson is the first US celebrity to admit to being infected with the disease.

2015 Researchers say a new, aggressive strain of HIV found in Cuba can progress victims to AIDS in two years instead of the usual ten.

1981
AIDS BREAKS OUT

As cases of AIDS broke out in America in 1981, *The New York Times* reported 41 cases of Kaposi's sarcoma found in gay men from New York City and San Francisco. By the end of the year, 270 cases of severe immune deficiency had been reported among homosexual American men, with 121 dying as a result. Gay leaders in Washington then lobbied the government to change the name of the disease from GRID (Gay-Related Immune Deficiency) to AIDS, as it was clearly not a gay-specific disease. The first case of AIDS was reported in the United Kingdom in 1981, followed by the first known cases in Italy, Brazil, Canada and Australia the following year.

1997
COMBINATION THERAPIES

In 1997, the first combination drug therapies with a high success rate against HIV were released to the public. Known as highly active antiretroviral therapies (HAART), the drugs worked by decreasing the patient's total burden of HIV, strengthening the immune system and preventing the opportunistic infections that often lead to AIDS and death. The combination therapies were so successful that in many parts of the world today the progression from HIV to AIDS has become increasingly rare. Despite this success rate, many prominent people died from AIDS during the 1990s, including singer Freddy Mercury, rapper Eazy-E, actor Anthony Perkins and author Isaac Asimov.

Freddie Mercury performing live on stage in July 1986.

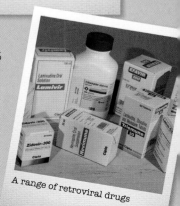

A range of retroviral drugs

1986
THE CHERNOBYL DISASTER

'The odds of a meltdown are one in 10,000 years. The plants have safe and reliable controls that are protected from any breakdown with three safety systems.'

– The Minister of Power and Electrification of Ukraine, Vitali Sklyarov, speaks to *Soviet Life* magazine about Ukraine's nuclear power stations

Events leading up to the explosion at Chernobyl, the worst disaster in the history of nuclear power, began during routine testing of the power station. In the early hours of 26 April 1986, night technicians at Chernobyl's number four reactor shut down its power regulating system and removed the control rods from its core. The reactor then experienced a power surge that caused it to overheat and set off several explosions. These led to a large explosion at 1.23am that blew the steel and concrete lid off the reactor, set the station on fire and caused a partial meltdown. A plume of smoke containing large amounts of radioactive debris then rose high into the atmosphere and blew north. Within a few days the nuclear fallout had passed over much of Europe. The Soviet Union attempted a cover-up, but Scandinavian monitoring stations that had recorded the fallout demanded to know what had happened. On 28 April, the Soviet government admitted there had been an explosion at Chernobyl and a public outcry in Europe ensued. Many people from the nearby city of Pripyat had watched the rising smoke from the power station, as firefighters desperately tried to put out the blaze. The next day, the residents of Pripyat went about their daily lives unaware of the danger. It took 36 hours after the explosion for an evacuation to be ordered. People from Pripyat and its outlying villages were then told to pack supplies for three days and to leave their pets behind. Many assumed they would be back within a few days but most of them would never return to their homes, which today make up the ghost town of Pripyat. Within three months, 31 people had died from the initial effects of Chernobyl, but the true legacy of its radioactive fallout is unknown. Conservative estimates put the death toll from Chernobyl-associated cancers and other diseases in the tens of thousands.

A bird's-eye view of Chernobyl's number four reactor, the source of the worst nuclear disaster in Europe.

FLASHPOINT FACT

The remains of Chernobyl's number four reactor will remain radioactive for 1,000 years.

TIMELINE

1970 Construction of the Chernobyl nuclear power plant and the nearby 'atom town' of Pripyat begins.

1982 A partial core meltdown occurs in Chernobyl's number one reactor, but the accident is covered up until 1986.

25 April 1986 A test begins on Chernobyl's number four reactor to observe the reactor under limited power flow.

1.35am, 26 April 1986 Firefighters arrive to fight the fires on the roof of the turbine hall.

6.35am, 26 April 1986 A total of 186 firefighters from 37 fire brigades extinguish all the fires except the one in the number four reactor.

1970	1976	1982	1983	1986	1986	1986	1986	1986

1976 Filling of the cooling water pools for the Chernobyl power plant begins.

1.23am, 26 April 1986 The reactor reaches 120 times its full power and explodes, firing radioactive debris into the atmosphere.

1983 The construction of Chernobyl's number four reactor is completed.

8pm, 26 April 1986 A government committee arrives to see pieces of graphite lying on the ground.

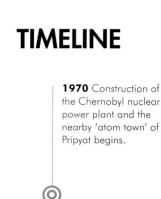

FLASHPOINTS

26 April 1986
BURNING GRAPHITE

Early in the morning of 26 April, hundreds of firefighters were called to contain the fire at the Chernobyl power station following the explosion. The attending firefighters and policemen noticed large pieces of graphite littered on the ground around Chernobyl, some of which were still red hot. However, despite record levels of radioactivity, nobody arriving at Chernobyl was issued with protective clothing. Nearby, people gathered on a railway bridge to watch the burning reactor. As these people commented on the rainbow colours caused by the burning graphite, they were exposed to a 500-roentgen dose of radiation. A dose of 750 roentgens is considered lethal. No-one who stood on the 'bridge of death' survived.

27 April 1986
HELICOPTER DROPS

At 10am on 27 April, helicopters began making drops of sand, lead, clay and neutron-absorbing boron onto Chernobyl's burning reactor, as the people of Pripyat were put on evacuation standby. However, of the 5,000 tonnes of material dropped on the reactor, almost none of the boron reached the core. One of the helicopters making the drops then collided with a crane and crashed, killing all four of its crew. By midday, the radiation levels had dropped enough at Chernobyl for authorities to re-evaluate an evacuation. But by 2pm radiation levels were up once more, and the 43,000 residents of Pripyat were evacuated aboard 1,200 buses.

Emergency crews at Chernobyl.

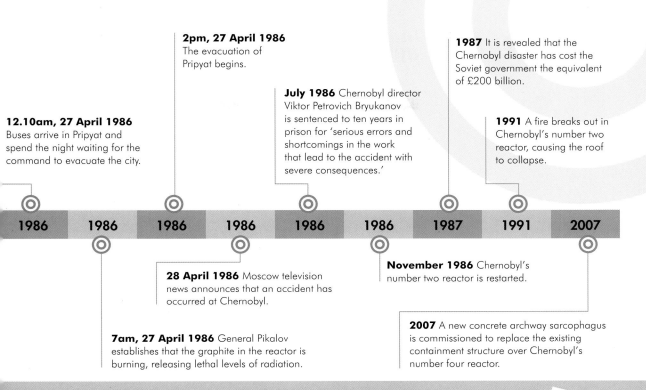

12.10am, 27 April 1986 Buses arrive in Pripyat and spend the night waiting for the command to evacuate the city.

2pm, 27 April 1986 The evacuation of Pripyat begins.

July 1986 Chernobyl director Viktor Petrovich Bryukanov is sentenced to ten years in prison for 'serious errors and shortcomings in the work that lead to the accident with severe consequences.'

1987 It is revealed that the Chernobyl disaster has cost the Soviet government the equivalent of £200 billion.

1991 A fire breaks out in Chernobyl's number two reactor, causing the roof to collapse.

1986	1986	1986	1986	1986	1986	1987	1991	2007

28 April 1986 Moscow television news announces that an accident has occurred at Chernobyl.

November 1986 Chernobyl's number two reactor is restarted.

7am, 27 April 1986 General Pikalov establishes that the graphite in the reactor is burning, releasing lethal levels of radiation.

2007 A new concrete archway sarcophagus is commissioned to replace the existing containment structure over Chernobyl's number four reactor.

May 1986
STEAM EXPLOSION

On 2 May, it was feared that molten graphite would reach the large pools beneath the still-burning reactor. It was thought that these pools, which were used as water reserves for the reactor's cooling pumps, could then create a steam explosion and eject more radioactive debris into the atmosphere. The three men who volunteered to drain the pools had to work underwater in total darkness, and died shortly afterwards from radiation poisoning. To reduce the risk of the molten reactor core mixing with water from the water table and creating a steam explosion, liquid nitrogen was pumped into the soil beneath the reactor. Thousands of Russian soldiers, known as 'bio-robots', were then brought in to collect the worst of the radioactive debris from the reactor. Many were exposed to over 100 times the radiation limits considered safe for humans, and died as a result.

December 1986
CONTAINMENT CONSTRUCTION

To prevent any further release of radioactive material, a concrete sarcophagus was built over the Chernobyl reactor in December 1986. Constructed from 300,000 tonnes of concrete and 6,000 tonnes of steel, the sarcophagus would supposedly protect the environment from radiation for at least 30 years. Construction of the sarcophagus was the biggest engineering project in history and involved 250,000 workers, all of whom reached their official lifetime limits of radiation during the job and received a medal for their efforts. The sarcophagus was later found to be structurally unsafe and leaking radiation. A new archway roof was commissioned in 2007 to replace it.

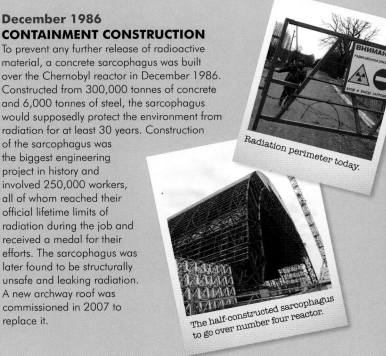

Radiation perimeter today.

The half-constructed sarcophagus to go over number four reactor.

1989
THE FALL OF THE BERLIN WALL

'Nobody has the intention of building a wall.'

– GDR head of state Walter Ulbricht speaks at a press conference in East Berlin on 15 June 1961, just weeks before barriers are erected between East and West Berlin

On the evening of 9 April 1989, an astonishing announcement was made on German television. During a press conference that day, East German official Günter Schabowski had declared that the checkpoint crossings in the Berlin Wall would be opened for the first time in 28 years. But when he was pressed on when this would take effect, Schabowski appeared flummoxed. He reread the note given to him by his party superiors and then replied, 'As far as I know, effective immediately, without delay.' It was a classic bureaucratic blunder: no-one had told Schabowski that the regulation was to come into force the next day, and suddenly, without warning, Schabowski had inadvertently all but announced the end of the Cold War. Tens of thousands of East Berliners subsequently flocked to the Berlin Wall checkpoint crossings, where confused guards, who knew nothing about the news, wondered how they would hold back the increasingly large crowd. In the end, just before 11pm, the

guards threw open the checkpoints and the first Berliners to pass freely from east to west in nearly three decades swarmed across the border. Here, they were met with champagne, joyful hugs and reunited family members, as the ecstatic crowd sang, cheered and climbed onto the wall in celebration. The festival atmosphere surrounding the fall of the Berlin Wall continued well into the next day, as East German army units began dismantling the wall to create more crossing points. Berliners cheered each other on as they attacked the wall with hammers and pickaxes, and took away large chunks as souvenirs. Crowds gathered again that week to watch bulldozers bring down large sections of the wall and reunite ancient Berlin roads. Today, only a few small sections of the Berlin Wall remain as sightseeing spots for tourists to visit. But few who were there will forget the moment the wall came down, heralding the end of the Cold War and the rapid decline of communist rule in Europe.

A modern tourist visits a graffitied section of the Berlin Wall: little of the wall remains standing today.

FLASHPOINT FACT

Before it was demolished, around 5,000 East Germans managed to cross the Berlin Wall safely, while another 5,000 were caught attempting to do so.
A total of 191 people were killed trying to cross the wall.

TIMELINE

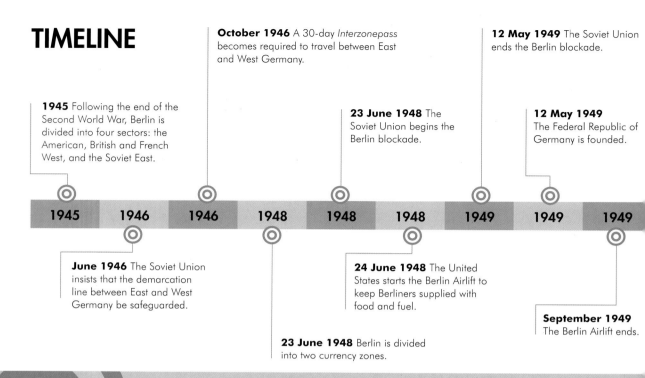

1945 Following the end of the Second World War, Berlin is divided into four sectors: the American, British and French West, and the Soviet East.

October 1946 A 30-day *Interzonepass* becomes required to travel between East and West Germany.

12 May 1949 The Soviet Union ends the Berlin blockade.

23 June 1948 The Soviet Union begins the Berlin blockade.

12 May 1949 The Federal Republic of Germany is founded.

1945	1946	1946	1948	1948	1948	1949	1949	1949

June 1946 The Soviet Union insists that the demarcation line between East and West Germany be safeguarded.

24 June 1948 The United States starts the Berlin Airlift to keep Berliners supplied with food and fuel.

September 1949 The Berlin Airlift ends.

23 June 1948 Berlin is divided into two currency zones.

FLASHPOINTS

1961
EAST–WEST DIVIDE

In 1949, Germany was divided into the Federal Republic of Germany, in the west, and the German Democratic Republic, in the east. This caused an exodus of around 2.5 million East Germans to the west between 1949 and 1961. Fearing it was losing its best and brightest workers to the democratic west, the GDR built a barrier in Berlin to close off access for East Germans. First erected on the night of 12 August, the original wall was constructed from barbed wire and cinder blocks, but these were later replaced by a series of 5-m (16-ft) high concrete walls topped with barbed wire, watchtowers and gun emplacements. By 1980, the Berlin Wall stretched for 45km (28 miles) through Berlin and extended for another 121km (75 miles) around West Berlin, cutting it off from East Germany.

May 1989
EAST MEETS WEST

In 1987, US president Ronald Regan asked Soviet Union leader Mikhail Gorbachev to tear down the Berlin Wall as a symbol of increasing freedom across Soviet Europe. In 1989, the Hungarian government dismantled the barbed-wire fences along its borders with Austria and thousands of East Germans illegally crossed into the country. Mass demonstrations then began in East Germany, the most notable of which was a large protest held by 500,000 people in East Berlin's Alexanderplatz. In reaction, East Germany's leader Erich Honecker resigned on 18 October 1989, and was replaced by Egon Krenz. Realizing that he could not stop the flow of East Germans escaping into Austria and Czechoslovakia, Krenz decided to allow border crossing between East and West Germany, including in Berlin. He left it to Günter Schabowski to announce the news

Construction begins on the Berlin Wall.

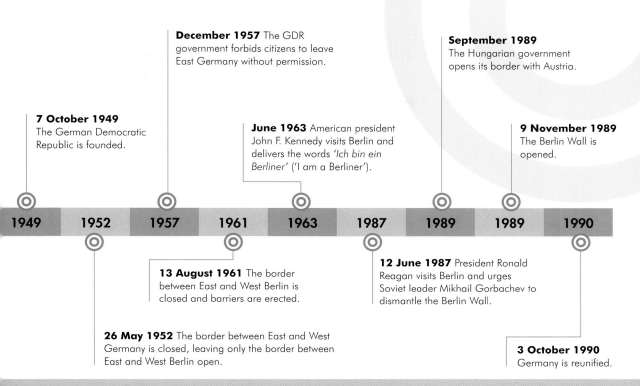

7 October 1949
The German Democratic Republic is founded.

December 1957 The GDR government forbids citizens to leave East Germany without permission.

June 1963 American president John F. Kennedy visits Berlin and delivers the words *'Ich bin ein Berliner'* ('I am a Berliner').

September 1989 The Hungarian government opens its border with Austria.

9 November 1989 The Berlin Wall is opened.

| 1949 | 1952 | 1957 | 1961 | 1963 | 1987 | 1989 | 1989 | 1990 |

13 August 1961 The border between East and West Berlin is closed and barriers are erected.

12 June 1987 President Ronald Reagan visits Berlin and urges Soviet leader Mikhail Gorbachev to dismantle the Berlin Wall.

26 May 1952 The border between East and West Germany is closed, leaving only the border between East and West Berlin open.

3 October 1990 Germany is reunified.

December 1989
THE COLD WAR ENDS

As the power of the Soviet Union in Europe began to crumble, an historic meeting took place between the leaders of the Cold War nations, the United States and the Soviet Union. On 3 December 1989, President George Bush met Soviet leader Mikhail Gorbachev aboard Soviet ship the SS *Maxim Gorkiy* off the coast of Malta. During this 'Malta Summit', the two leaders agreed to officially end the Cold War that had begun four decades earlier and at times threatened to plunge the world into nuclear devastation. Pieces of the Berlin Wall were handed out by Bush at the end of the summit.

October 1990
GERMANY REUNIFIES

In July 1990, East Germany formally adopted the currency of West Germany and all border controls between the two halves of the country ended. This marked the start of German reunification, which reached its conclusion 95 days later on 3 October 1990. Not everyone was happy about the reunification: British prime minister Margaret Thatcher had asked Gorbachev to stop it happening, saying it would undermine the security of Europe. French president François Mitterrand had also voiced his concern, telling Thatcher that a reunified Germany could potentially be more dangerous than Nazi Germany. The people of Germany disagreed and came out in force on 9 November 1990 to celebrate the one-year anniversary of the fall of the Berlin Wall, and the birth of a new democratic Europe.

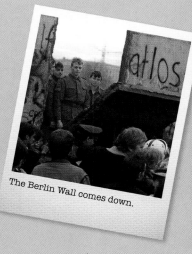
The Berlin Wall comes down.

1989
THE TIANANMEN SQUARE MASSACRE

'If some so-called democratic fighters seize power, they'll start fighting among themselves. As soon as civil war breaks out, there will be rivers of blood.'

– Chinese leader Deng Xiaoping justifies his decision to sanction a violent military suppression of student demonstrations in Tiananmen Square

The lone man looked small and unassuming as he stood, dressed in black trousers, a white shirt and apparently carrying his shopping, before an approaching column of Chinese tanks. As the first tank swerved to the side, the man stepped into its path. As it swerved in the other direction, the man again blocked its way. Then he clambered on to the vehicle to speak to the driver, although his exact words are unknown. The image of this man standing up to the mighty war machinery of the Chinese Communist Party (CCP) became the iconic image of the 1989 Tiananmen Square Massacre – the night when soldiers fired indiscriminately on a crowd of protestors in Beijing. The protest had begun to mourn the death of Hu Yaobang, a former general secretary of the CCP, and one of the few party members open to democratic reform. The 10,000 mourners, mostly made up of university students, gathered in Tiananmen Square to grieve and protest. Days of rolling demonstrations followed as protesting crowds across China called for political, social and economic reforms. On the day of a state visit by Mikhail Gorbachev, over one million people descended on Tiananmen Square and their protest was captured by the world's media. The enraged and embarrassed CCP responded by declaring martial law. Then, on the night of 3 June, tanks, helicopters and tens of thousands of troops armed with assault rifles advanced on Tiananmen Square. The soldiers moved slowly towards the centre of the square to surround the protestors there, pausing only to kneel and fire into the crowd. After hours of violence between soldiers and protestors, the army had won control of the square by late morning. As the army cemented its suppression of the protestors on 5 June, the international media captured the most enduring image of the Tiananmen Square Massacre: a lone man standing before a column of tanks.

Students from Tiananmen Square cart away an injured protestor after Chinese soldiers fire indiscriminately on the crowd.

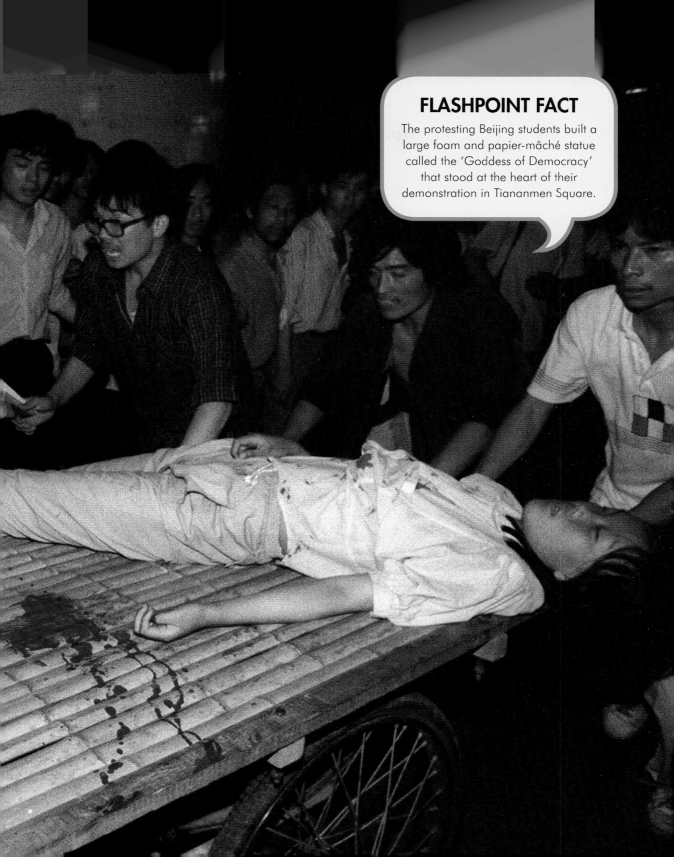

TIMELINE

December 1986 The first student demonstrations are held in Beijing, calling for economic liberalization and democratic rule.

15 April 1989 Mourners gather in Tiananmen Square following Hu Yaobang's death.

22 April 1989 Tens of thousands of students gather outside the Great Hall of the People in Tiananmen Square for Hu Yaobang's memorial.

27 April 1989 Between 50,000 and 100,000 Beijing students march to Tiananmen Square.

4 May 1989 Tens of thousands of Chinese students in cities nationwide stage the biggest pro-democracy demonstration ever held in China.

| 1986 | 1987 | 1989 | 1989 | 1989 | 1989 | 1989 | 1989 | 1989 |

January 1987 Hu Yaobang is forced to resign as CCP general secretary for taking a soft stance against the protests.

26 April 1989 An inflammatory editorial in the state-run newspaper, *The People's Daily*, accuses the protestors of anti-communist activity.

11 May 1989 Ahead of a visit by Soviet leader Mikhail Gorbachev, hundreds of students begin a hunger strike in Tiananmen Square.

18–21 April 1989 Numbers in Beijing swell into the thousands as demonstrations spread to cities and universities nationwide.

FLASHPOINTS

26 April 1989
SUPPRESSING STANCE

Outraged by the protests in Tiananmen Square, a debate raged in the CCP about the appropriate action to take. Hu Yaobang's successor as party general secretary, Zhao Ziyang, advocated taking a diplomatic path with the protestors. However, this stance was overruled by Chinese premier Li Peng and hardline party leader Deng Xiaoping, who insisted that the protestors be forcibly suppressed. Deng Xiaoping then officially denounced the protest on 26 April. Zhao Ziyang made a last appeal to the protesting students for a peaceful end to their demonstrations in May. He was removed from power shortly afterwards.

13 May 1989
HUNGER STRIKE

Two days before a much-publicized visit by Mikhail Gorbachev, students occupying Tiananmen Square began a hunger strike. It was well known that international media outlets would be in Beijing to report on the Gorbachev visit, and a hunger strike would help to spread their message around the world. Sympathetic citizens, including Buddhist monks, flocked to the square in support of the students, which further raised the profile of the hunger strike. As the Red Cross sent in medical teams and supplies to help the students, the CCP was forced to cancel a planned welcoming ceremony for Gorbachev in Tiananmen Square.

The occupation of Tiananmen Square.

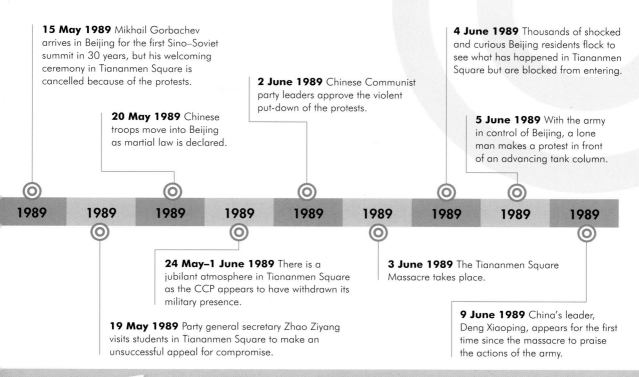

15 May 1989 Mikhail Gorbachev arrives in Beijing for the first Sino–Soviet summit in 30 years, but his welcoming ceremony in Tiananmen Square is cancelled because of the protests.

20 May 1989 Chinese troops move into Beijing as martial law is declared.

2 June 1989 Chinese Communist party leaders approve the violent put-down of the protests.

4 June 1989 Thousands of shocked and curious Beijing residents flock to see what has happened in Tiananmen Square but are blocked from entering.

5 June 1989 With the army in control of Beijing, a lone man makes a protest in front of an advancing tank column.

1989 1989 1989 1989 1989 1989 1989 1989 1989

24 May–1 June 1989 There is a jubilant atmosphere in Tiananmen Square as the CCP appears to have withdrawn its military presence.

19 May 1989 Party general secretary Zhao Ziyang visits students in Tiananmen Square to make an unsuccessful appeal for compromise.

3 June 1989 The Tiananmen Square Massacre takes place.

9 June 1989 China's leader, Deng Xiaoping, appears for the first time since the massacre to praise the actions of the army.

Martial law is declared.

20 May 1989
MARTIAL LAW

On 20 May, the CCP declared martial law in Beijing. Over 250,000 soldiers were sent to the capital to take control of the streets, but they were blocked at the city's outlying suburbs by throngs of protestors. The protestors then surrounded the soldiers and appealed to them to join their cause. The army had no choice but to withdraw its troops and tanks, although this apparent backing down was only to prepare for the 3 June assault on Tiananmen Square.

9 June 1989
GOVERNMENT PRAISE

In the week following the army's seizure of Tiananmen Square, the government began a purge against officials who had condoned the protests as well as jailing the students who had organized them. On 9 June, Deng Xiaoping made a speech praising the army and the successful suppression of the protestors. Several foreign journalists who had covered the massacre were expelled from China and blacklisted from re-entering. Journalists reporting on the massacre had estimated that between 400 and 1,000 protestors had been killed, but the Chinese Red Cross put the death toll at 2,600, although it later retracted this figure. The CCP said that between 200 and 300 people had been killed. Today, all forms of discussion or remembrance of the Tiananmen Square Massacre are prohibited in China.

1991

TIM BERNERS-LEE LAUNCHES THE WORLD WIDE WEB

'There was a time when people felt the Internet was another world, but now people realize it's a tool that we use in this world.'

— Tim Berners-Lee discusses the development of the World Wide Web

Tim Berners-Lee was a little-known software engineer when he conceived a new way of sharing information that is today known as the World Wide Web. At the time, Berners-Lee worked in Geneva, Switzerland for CERN, the European Organization for Nuclear Research. Scientists from around the world worked at CERN for limited periods, conducting experiments before travelling home to their own laboratories. An important part of their work was to share research data and results with other CERN scientists, but there was no common hardware or software that would enable this. Recognizing a gap in communications technology, Berners-Lee wrote a proposal on 12 March 1989 for a worldwide database that married hypertext with the Internet to create a mutually accessible 'web' of information. The Internet had been used by companies to share information since the early 1980s, but hypertext was the key that made the Internet accessible within a global context. Calling this new system the

World Wide Web, Berners-Lee launched the first website, http://info.cern.ch, on 6 August 1991. This explained the concept of the World Wide Web and provided the first Web browser and editor so that people could build their own websites. The Web as we know it today was born. The World Wide Web became rapidly accepted with the creation of a graphical web browser called 'Mosiac', which allowed users the same 'point-and-click' mechanism that had been used on personal computers for some years. In 1994, the Netscape web browser was released and it quickly became the dominant browser that made the Web widely accessible. By the mid-1990s, the Web had millions of daily users. Since then, the World Wide Web has grown into the greatest communication tool the world has ever known. It has enabled the rapid exchange of information that has changed the way we collect information, communicate with each other, buy and sell, and spend our leisure time.

Part of the enormous ENIAC computer.

FLASHPOINT FACT
The World Wide Web was almost called the Mine of Information, The Information Mine or The Mesh, but inventor Tim Berners-Lee didn't think they 'had quite the right ring'.

TIMELINE

1964 Douglas Engelbart unveils a prototype of the modern computer with a mouse and a graphical user interface.

1976 Steve Jobs and Steve Wozniak found Apple Computers.

1953 Grace Hopper develops the first computer language, later known as 'COBOL'.

1975 The IBM 5100 becomes the first commercially available portable computer.

1989 Tim Berners-Lee proposes the World Wide Web.

| 1953 | 1958 | 1964 | 1971 | 1975 | 1975 | 1976 | 1977 | 1989 | 1991 |

1958 Jack Kilby and Robert Noyce create the integrated circuit, or 'computer chip'.

April 1975 Microsoft is founded by Bill Gates and Paul Allen to develop programs for the build-it-yourself Altair 880 personal computer.

1991 The first World Wide Web pages appear.

1971 IBM engineers invent the 'floppy disk', which allows data to be shared among computers.

1977 The Apple II is unveiled.

FLASHPOINTS

1945
THE FIRST DIGITAL COMPUTER

Commissioned by the US military in 1943, the Electronic Numerical Integrator and Computer (ENIAC) was the first programmable general-purpose electronic digital computer. Filling an entire room, ENIAC was the most powerful calculating device built to date and included many of the fundamental concepts and components that are used in modern computers today. ENIAC could make calculations in 30 seconds that would take a human 20 hours, and was immediately put to calculating the trajectories of ballistic missiles. However, as is the case today, computing technology moved quickly in the late 1940s, and by 1952 ENIAC had become all but obsolete. In 1955, what was once the fastest computer in the world was shut down for good. But its creation would lead to home computers that could communicate with each other via the World Wide Web within 40 years.

1962
THE INTERNET

In 1962, the American Department of Defense's Advanced Research Projects Agency (ARPA) proposed a 'galactic network' of computers that could talk to one another. This would enable US military forces to communicate with each other if a Soviet Union attack brought down the nation's phone lines. The subsequent system became known as the 'ARPAnet', and in 1969 it delivered its first message between a computer at Stanford University and one at UCLA. Both computers were the size of a room and crashed after sending the first two letters of the first message: 'LOGIN'. In the 1970s, computers from the University of Hawaii and London's University College were added to the network. By the end of the 1970s, a computer scientist named Vinton Cerf found a way for more computers to join the network and communicate successfully. The Internet was born.

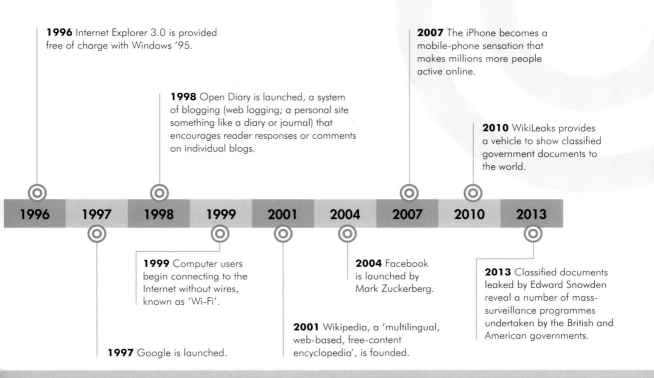

1996 Internet Explorer 3.0 is provided free of charge with Windows '95.

1998 Open Diary is launched, a system of blogging (web logging; a personal site something like a diary or journal) that encourages reader responses or comments on individual blogs.

2007 The iPhone becomes a mobile-phone sensation that makes millions more people active online.

2010 WikiLeaks provides a vehicle to show classified government documents to the world.

| 1996 | 1997 | 1998 | 1999 | 2001 | 2004 | 2007 | 2010 | 2013 |

1999 Computer users begin connecting to the Internet without wires, known as 'Wi-Fi'.

2004 Facebook is launched by Mark Zuckerberg.

2013 Classified documents leaked by Edward Snowden reveal a number of mass-surveillance programmes undertaken by the British and American governments.

1997 Google is launched.

2001 Wikipedia, a 'multilingual, web-based, free-content encyclopedia', is founded.

1975
FIRST PERSONAL COMPUTERS

In 1975, the Altair 8800 microcomputer kit was released to the American public. Altair enabled home-electronics enthusiasts to assemble their own home computers rather than shell out the $15,000 it cost to buy a preassembled model from IBM. By 1981, several companies competed for dominance of the personal computer (PC) market, but when IBM released a model for under $2,000 that included floppy-disk drives and 64kb of memory, it held sway over consumers. By licencing its operating system from a little-known software company called Microsoft, the IBM PC had the edge over its competition in the computer wars of the 1980s. In a few short years, PC users would be accessing the World Wide Web for the first time.

1980
ENQUIRE

While working at CERN in 1980, Tim Berners-Lee wrote a software program called ENQUIRE, which was the predecessor to the World Wide Web. Berners-Lee recognized that the 10,000 people working at CERN needed to share information electronically, but their different hardware and software systems were making this impossible. ENQUIRE aimed to cross these boundaries by introducing a common hypertext publishing format that could link documents and other resources. In 1989, Berners-Lee published a paper called 'Information Management: A Proposal' that suggested combining hypertext with the Internet to create an information 'web' that he called the World Wide Web.

Sir Timothy Berners-Lee, inventor of the World Wide Web.

Profile

NELSON MANDELA

Nelson Mandela, the father of democracy in South Africa.

'If you want to make peace with your enemy, you have to work with your enemy. Then he becomes your partner.'

– Nelson Mandela speaks about reconciliation after being freed from prison

Nelson Mandela and his wife Winnie celebrate his release from prison after 27 years inside.

When Nelson Mandela was released from his 27-year imprisonment, he did not seek revenge or retribution against his white oppressors, but reconciliation. In 1964, Mandela had been sentenced for treason against the state and narrowly avoided the death penalty. By incarcerating the leader of the African National Congress (ANC), the government of South Africa though it could silence opposition to its apartheid rule. Instead, Mandela became a symbol for the fight against apartheid, which led to his eventual release and the abandonment of the apartheid system. Apartheid, or 'apart-hood', was introduced in 1948 by the National Party and relegated black South Africans to lives of servitude. Mandela began his struggle against it when he joined the ANC as a law student in Johannesburg and helped found its youth league. Although advocating a policy of non-violent protests, Mandela was repeatedly arrested for seditious activities, which led to his unsuccessful prosecution in the Treason Trial of 1956. However, Mandela put aside civil disobedience following the 1960 Sharpeville Massacre, which left 69 protestors dead when they were fired on by police. The government declared a state of emergency and banned the ANC. In response, Mandela sought out military support for the party in other countries. On his return, he was arrested and imprisoned. Over the next 27 years, international pressure, boycotts and economic sanctions helped to force the government into freeing him. Mandela's release would see the end of apartheid, the first multiracial elections in South Africa and his swearing in as president. After 300 years of white rule, Mandela's inauguration speech did not urge wrath or rancour, but truth, reconciliation and the unification of black and white South Africans. At the time of his death, Mandela was a symbol for democracy, freedom, human rights and the fight against oppression.

FLASHPOINT FACT

Mandela won more than 250 awards after his release from prison, including the 1993 Nobel Peace Prize.

TIMELINE

1918 Rolihlahla (later Nelson) Mandela is born at Mvezo in South Africa's Transkei.

1941 Mandela escapes an arranged marriage and begins working at the law firm Witkin, Sidelsky and Eidelman.

1944 Mandela co-founds the ANC Youth League (ANCYL) and marries Evelyn Ntoko Mase.

1952 Mandela is elected president of the ANCYL.

1956 Mandela is arrested for treason along with 155 other members of the African National Congress. All are acquitted by 29 March.

1961 Mandela goes underground and forms the militant *Umkhonto we Sizwe*, or 'Spear of the Nation'.

1918	1939	1941	1944	1952	1952	1956	1958	1960	1961

1952 As the campaign of defiance begins, Mandela is arrested and charged for violating the Suppression of Communism Act. Mandela is sentenced to nine months imprisonment with hard labour, suspended for two years.

1960 The ANC is banned after the Sharpeville Massacre.

1939 Mandela enrols at the University College of Fort Hare.

1958 Mandela divorces Evelyn Mase and marries Nomzamo 'Winnie' Madikizela.

FLASHPOINTS

1918
TRIBAL BEGINNINGS

Mandela was born in 1918, in South Africa's Transkei, to a chieftain of the Tembu people. Mandela's childhood was split between his tribal roots and a growing desire for a modern English life. He was given the tribal forename 'Rolihlahla', a Xhosa term that means 'troublemaker', but he was commonly known as Nelson, a name given to him by his teacher. Rejecting his family's wishes for an arranged marriage, Mandela went to Johannesburg and graduated with a law degree in 1942. His political activism began in 1943, when he marched for a bus boycott to reverse a bus-fair rise. Mandela then joined the ANC and co-founded its Youth League in 1944. In 1953, Mandela and long-time friend and collaborator, Oliver Tambo, set up South Africa's first black law firm, which offered legal advice to black people.

1952
NON-VIOLENCE

From 1952, Mandela advocated similar methods of civil disobedience used by Gandhi against British rule in India, including strikes and street marches. Thousands gathered to hear Mandela speak about his campaign against the government, including during a rally in Durban that saw Mandela briefly imprisoned. As Mandela's protests grew so did the ANC membership, which increased from 20,000 to 100,000 within a matter of months. In response, the government ordered mass arrests and introduced martial law through the Public Safety Act of 1953. By 1956, Mandela considered revising his non-violent methods to include a more direct militant approach. This he put into practice following the Sharpeville Massacre of 1960, which also led to his arrest in 1964 and imprisonment for 27 years.

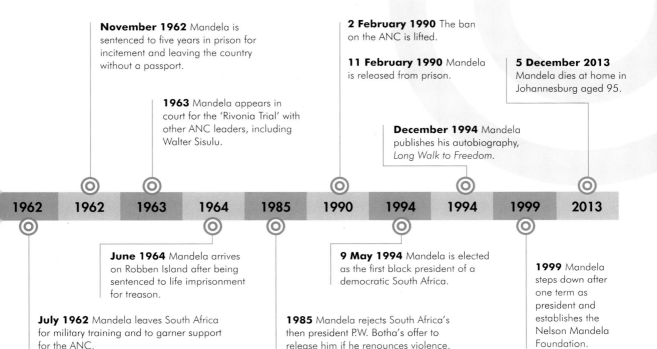

November 1962 Mandela is sentenced to five years in prison for incitement and leaving the country without a passport.

1963 Mandela appears in court for the 'Rivonia Trial' with other ANC leaders, including Walter Sisulu.

2 February 1990 The ban on the ANC is lifted.

11 February 1990 Mandela is released from prison.

5 December 2013 Mandela dies at home in Johannesburg aged 95.

December 1994 Mandela publishes his autobiography, *Long Walk to Freedom*.

| 1962 | 1962 | 1963 | 1964 | 1985 | 1990 | 1994 | 1994 | 1999 | 2013 |

June 1964 Mandela arrives on Robben Island after being sentenced to life imprisonment for treason.

July 1962 Mandela leaves South Africa for military training and to garner support for the ANC.

9 May 1994 Mandela is elected as the first black president of a democratic South Africa.

1985 Mandela rejects South Africa's then president P.W. Botha's offer to release him if he renounces violence.

1999 Mandela steps down after one term as president and establishes the Nelson Mandela Foundation.

Mandela's cell on Robben Island.

1990
ROAD TO FREEDOM

In 1989, F.W. de Klerk became the president of South Africa and called for the abandonment of apartheid. He lifted the government's previous ban on protest marches and abolished elements of apartheid such as segregated public spaces. When de Klerk released ANC leader Walter Sisulu in 1989, it looked as though change was to become a reality. This was confirmed on 11 February 1990, when Nelson Mandela was released from prison. On 4 May, while violence in black homelands raged in the background, Mandela met with de Klerk to discuss how to bring about stability.

1994
MULTIRACIAL ELECTIONS

On 27 April 1994, millions of black South Africans took up their right to vote for the first time in the country's first democratic general election. Nelson Mandela won by a landslide margin to become South Africa's first black president. Known in South Africa as 'the founding father of democracy', Mandela stood down from the presidency in 1999. One of the most recognizable figures in the world, Mandela continued to use his fame to promote good causes, including raising awareness of the deadly HIV/AIDS virus. He died on 5 December 2013 at the age of 95, leading to widespread mourning.

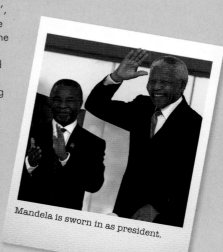

Mandela is sworn in as president.

1991

THE COLLAPSE OF THE SOVIET UNION

'A society should never become like a pond with stagnant water, without movement. That's the most important thing.'

– Mikhail Gorbachev talks about reforming the Soviet model

On 25 December 1991, the red hammer-and-sickle flag was lowered from the Kremlin for the last time, as Soviet leader Mikhail Gorbachev resigned. The world looked on in amazement as the Soviet Union officially ended. The collapse had been imminent following an attempted coup by communist hardliners in August, a last-ditch effort to restore party rule to the country and undo Gorbachev's democratic reforms. Gorbachev had inherited a stalled economy when he came to power in 1985 and had instituted the reconstructive policies known as *glasnost* and *perestroika*. *Glasnost* introduced political openness and did away with Stalinist repression. New freedoms were granted to Soviet citizens, political prisoners were released and newspapers could be critical of government policy. *Perestroika* brought about economic reform by loosening the government's stranglehold on the economy. For the first time, citizens were allowed to start private businesses, workers were granted the right to strike and

foreign investment was encouraged. These new policies brought a profound change, which created breakthrough historical moments such as Gorbachev and President Bush meeting in 1989 to declare the end of the Cold War. However, Gorbachev's new market economy was slow to bear fruit. While the west praised Gorbachev's reforms, his people suffered food shortages at home. As Gorbachev reduced the Soviet military presence among the Warsaw Pact nations of eastern Europe, they too expressed their dissatisfaction. The first revolution took place in Poland, where in 1989 they won the right to hold free elections. Czechoslovakia was next to overthrow its communist government, and one by one the nations of eastern Europe began to declare their independence from Moscow. In December 1991, Belarus, Russia and the Ukraine entered the Commonwealth of Independent States (CIS) and a few weeks later they were joined by the remaining republics. The Soviet Union had fallen.

The Soviet Communist party tries in vain to assert its authority by instigating a military coup in Moscow.

FLASHPOINT FACT

After the fall of the Soviet Union, countries such as Ukraine and Belarus retained control over the Soviet nuclear weapons that had been left on their soil.

TIMELINE

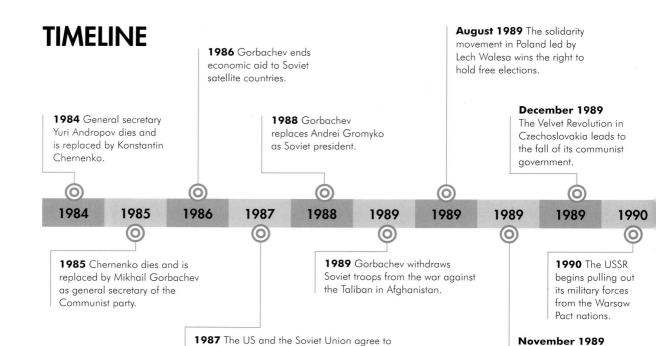

1984 General secretary Yuri Andropov dies and is replaced by Konstantin Chernenko.

1986 Gorbachev ends economic aid to Soviet satellite countries.

1988 Gorbachev replaces Andrei Gromyko as Soviet president.

August 1989 The solidarity movement in Poland led by Lech Walesa wins the right to hold free elections.

December 1989 The Velvet Revolution in Czechoslovakia leads to the fall of its communist government.

| 1984 | 1985 | 1986 | 1987 | 1988 | 1989 | 1989 | 1989 | 1989 | 1990 |

1985 Chernenko dies and is replaced by Mikhail Gorbachev as general secretary of the Communist party.

1989 Gorbachev withdraws Soviet troops from the war against the Taliban in Afghanistan.

1990 The USSR begins pulling out its military forces from the Warsaw Pact nations.

1987 The US and the Soviet Union agree to scrap intermediate-range nuclear missiles.

November 1989 The Berlin Wall falls.

FLASHPOINTS

19 August 1991
COMMUNIST COUP

On 19 August 1991, hardline communist members of the government started a military coup by placing Gorbachev under house arrest and issuing an emergency decree that suspended all political activity. As tanks rolled into Moscow, its inhabitants flocked to the Russian parliament building to protect it from attack. Boris Yeltsin, president of the Russian Soviet Federative Socialist Republic (RSFSR), then climbed aboard a tank and implored the soldiers not to fire on the unarmed people of Moscow. As he denounced the coup as an act of terror, his speech was broadcast around the world. It represented the popular will of the Soviet people not to return to a Stalinist society.

20 August 1991
BREAKING CURFEW

On 20 August, the military declared a curfew would take effect in Moscow. This was treated as a sign that the military was about to attack the parliament building, the White House. In response, thousands of Moscow citizens began building barricades around the White House and prepared for the tanks to begin firing. However, no attack came that day. Instead, at around 1am the next morning, armoured vehicles approached the White House but were unable to pass by the parked buses and cleaning vehicles blocking their way. The military was ordered to retreat: the coup was over.

Gorbachev after his release from house arrest.

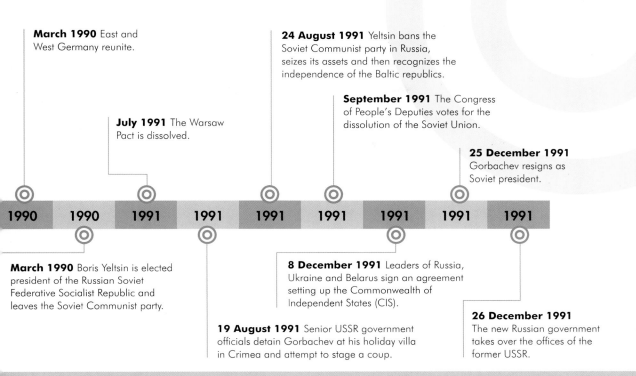

March 1990 East and West Germany reunite.

July 1991 The Warsaw Pact is dissolved.

24 August 1991 Yeltsin bans the Soviet Communist party in Russia, seizes its assets and then recognizes the independence of the Baltic republics.

September 1991 The Congress of People's Deputies votes for the dissolution of the Soviet Union.

25 December 1991 Gorbachev resigns as Soviet president.

| 1990 | 1990 | 1991 | 1991 | 1991 | 1991 | 1991 | 1991 | 1991 |

March 1990 Boris Yeltsin is elected president of the Russian Soviet Federative Socialist Republic and leaves the Soviet Communist party.

8 December 1991 Leaders of Russia, Ukraine and Belarus sign an agreement setting up the Commonwealth of Independent States (CIS).

19 August 1991 Senior USSR government officials detain Gorbachev at his holiday villa in Crimea and attempt to stage a coup.

26 December 1991 The new Russian government takes over the offices of the former USSR.

24 August 1991
YELTSIN IN CONTROL

With the coup over, Gorbachev flew back to Moscow. But here, Boris Yeltsin, the main figure in the resistance to the coup, was already making changes. Although the Russian constitution did not empower the president of the RSFSR with such authority, Yeltsin took advantage of the chaos caused by the coup to push for an end to communist rule. With the support of the people on Yeltsin's side, Gorbachev had little choice but to resign as Communist party secretary. The next day, Yeltsin met with the leaders of Belarus and the Ukraine to announce the end of the Soviet Union.

25 December 1991
INDEPENDENCE

On 24 December 1991, the Russian Federation informed the United Nations that it would succeed the Soviet Union in its UN membership. None of the member states objected. After the succession of Russia, Gorbachev announced his resignation as Soviet president on 25 December. The Soviet flag was lowered from the Kremlin roof and replaced with the new tricolour flag of Russia. What had been the USSR became 15 separate countries that agreed to collaborate as the new Commonwealth of Independent States (CIS).

The tricolour flag of Russia.

Boris Yeltsin celebrates the fall of communism.

1997
THE KYOTO TREATY

'The conversation on global warming has been stalled because a shrinking group of denialists fly into a rage when it's mentioned.'

– Environmentalist Al Gore discusses why he thinks climate-change reforms have taken so long

Towards the end of the 20th century, governments from around the world were forced to acknowledge one of the most pressing issues facing the planet: climate change. From the 1980s, scientists had warned the world about global warming, a phenomenon in part brought about by the emission of greenhouse gases from human activity. The human combustion of fossil fuels, which rapidly accelerated at the time of the Industrial Revolution, is responsible for steady increases in various greenhouse gases, particularly carbon dioxide, methane, ozone and chlorofluorocarbons. In 1997, representatives from 41 nations of the world gathered in Kyoto, Japan, to adopt a legal document agreeing to reduce six greenhouse gases, including carbon dioxide and methane. This subsequent 'Kyoto Protocol', which came into force in 2005, aimed to reduce emissions in countries to 5.2 per cent below 1990 levels during the 'commitment period' of 2008 to 2012. Countries of the European Union, for example, were set

A view of Shanghai through the smog. Today, the largest Chinese city is one of the most polluted cities in the world.

the task of reducing their emissions by an average of eight per cent, while Canada's reduction target was six per cent. The protocol, which made up part of the United Nations Framework Convention on Climate Change, was widely believed to be the most significant treaty on climate change created. Critics of the protocol, however, say that it has been highly ineffective. Many countries have not met their emission targets, while others have simply withdrawn from the treaty. President George W. Bush pulled America out of the treaty in 2001 because he said it would undermine the US economy, while pointing out that the emerging industrial nations of China and India were not even involved. At the end of 2012, an agreement was reached to extend the protocol to 2020, when a new successor document will be put in place. Today, 192 nations are signed to the protocol and, despite the rise of global emissions worldwide, environmentalists often support the Kyoto Protocol because it is 'the only game in town'.

FLASHPOINT FACT

Humans release around 30 billion metric tonnes of carbon dioxide (CO_2) into the atmosphere each year.

TIMELINE

1958 The first atmospheric CO$_2$ testing at Mauna Loa in Hawaii provides the first proof that CO$_2$ concentrations are rising.

1972 The first UN environment conference is held in Stockholm, Sweden.

1990 The IPCC produces its first assessment report, showing that temperatures have risen by 0.3–0.6°C over the last century.

1987 The Montreal Protocol, which restricts chemicals that damage the ozone layer, is agreed.

1992 The Earth Summit is held in Rio de Janeiro.

1958	1965	1972	1975	1987	1988	1990	1992	1997

1965 A US Advisory Committee warns that the greenhouse effect is a matter of 'real concern'.

1988 The Intergovernmental Panel on Climate Change (IPCC) is formed to collate and assess evidence on climate change.

1997 The Kyoto Protocol is agreed.

1975 American scientist Wallace Broecker coins the term 'global warming'.

1992
EARTH SUMMIT

In June 1992, representatives from 116 countries gathered in Rio de Janeiro for the United Nations Conference on Environment and Development (UNCED), also known as the 'Earth Summit'. The summit was designed as a first meeting of the United Nations Framework Convention on Climate Change (UNFCCC), formed to 'stabilize greenhouse gas concentrations in the atmosphere at a level that would prevent dangerous anthropogenic interference with the climate system.' As the purpose of the Earth Summit was to establish the working aims of the UNFCCC, no limits were imposed on greenhouse-gas emissions by individual nations. Instead, specific international treaties, called protocols, would be arranged at subsequent meetings.

2012
DOHA AMENDMENT

In 2012, a second Kyoto Protocol commitment period was agreed at a UN Climate Change Conference in Doha, Qatar. Known as the Doha Amendment, this second round of gas-emission cuts targeted 15 per cent of global gas emissions and committed participants to cut their emissions by an average of 18 per cent by 2020. Overall, the Doha Amendment laid out binding greenhouse-gas emission targets for 37 countries and by May 2015, 30 countries had ratified the agreement. However, even fewer countries overall were bound to the second period than the first, leading critics to call the Kyoto extension a pyrrhic victory.

The 2012 UN Climate Change Conference in Doha, Qatar.

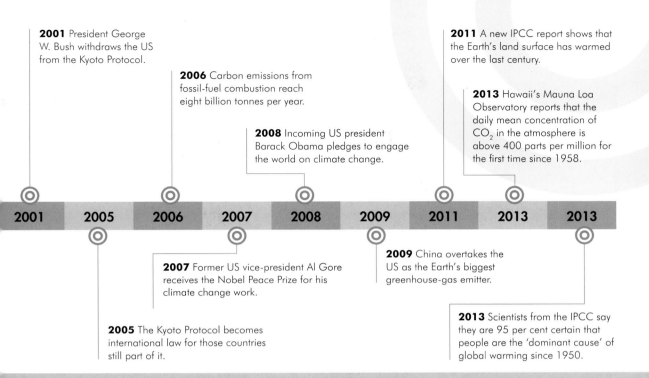

2001 President George W. Bush withdraws the US from the Kyoto Protocol.

2006 Carbon emissions from fossil-fuel combustion reach eight billion tonnes per year.

2008 Incoming US president Barack Obama pledges to engage the world on climate change.

2011 A new IPCC report shows that the Earth's land surface has warmed over the last century.

2013 Hawaii's Mauna Loa Observatory reports that the daily mean concentration of CO_2 in the atmosphere is above 400 parts per million for the first time since 1958.

| 2001 | 2005 | 2006 | 2007 | 2008 | 2009 | 2011 | 2013 | 2013 |

2007 Former US vice-president Al Gore receives the Nobel Peace Prize for his climate change work.

2009 China overtakes the US as the Earth's biggest greenhouse-gas emitter.

2005 The Kyoto Protocol becomes international law for those countries still part of it.

2013 Scientists from the IPCC say they are 95 per cent certain that people are the 'dominant cause' of global warming since 1950.

2012
KYOTO RESULTS

Under the Kyoto Protocol of 1997, most developed nations committed to reducing their greenhouse-gas emissions. The average target was a cut of around five per cent between 2008 and 2012. However, the results by 2012 were extremely poor. Europe as a whole only reduced its emissions by around one per cent, while between 1990 and 2008, its global emissions increased by seven per cent. The protocol's disappointing results were not helped by the 2001 withdrawal of the United States, which contributed 36 per cent of global greenhouse-gas emissions in 1990. Canada also withdrew from the protocol in 2011, saying that it was nowhere near meeting its emissions target. Canada's 2009 emissions were 17 per cent higher than in 1990. Although the countries of the Kyoto Protocol had not met their targets, the protocol was still hailed as a first step to establishing climate diplomacy around the world.

2014
GREEN CLIMATE FUND

In 2011, a United Nations Climate Change Conference held in Durban, South Africa agreed to set up a Green Climate Fund for developing nations. The fund aims to help these nations invest in green energy and technology, and enable them to fend off the impacts of climate change by building defences against rising seas, storms, floods and droughts. The fund was greatly helped in November 2014, when 30 nations agreed to donate $9.3 billion to the Green Climate Fund. The fund earmarked the first of the money for grants and loans for projects such as tree planting, wind and solar farms and disaster proofing.

Delegation members from around 170 countries.

1997
SCIENTISTS CLONE DOLLY

'Dolly is derived from a mammary gland cell and we couldn't think of a more impressive pair of glands than Dolly Parton's.'

– Dr Ian Wilmut explains the rationale behind the name of the sheep clone, Dolly

At the beginning of the 20th century, artificially creating life was a concept only explored by science fiction and gothic literature. However, by the end of the century, humans had found a way of cloning mammals. An example of this new scientific sensation was unveiled in 1997 in the form of Dolly the sheep. Dolly was different from the various other organisms that had been cloned in the years leading up to her birth on 5 July 1996, because she had been successfully cloned from an adult cell instead of from an embryo cell. To create Dolly, a mammary gland cell was taken from one ewe and fused with a second ewe's unfertilized egg cell, which had had its nucleus removed. When the egg cell developed into an embryo it was transplanted into a surrogate mother, which then carried out a normal pregnancy and gave birth to Dolly. Dolly's birth was greeted with a frenzy of amazement, controversy and speculation

Dr Ian Wilmut of the Roslin Institute in Scotland feeds Dolly the cloned sheep, his creation.

about the future of cloning. For many, animal cloning raised ethical questions about how far humans should be allowed to interfere with the creation of life. Many feared that the birth of Dolly meant that human cloning was just around the corner. In the US, President Bill Clinton ordered that a task force be set up to explore the legal and ethical implications of cloning. Clinton's predecessor, George W. Bush, made it known that he was repelled by the idea of human cloning, even for use in medical research. Dr Ian Wilmut himself, the Scottish scientist behind Dolly's birth, described human cloning as 'repugnant'. Many scientists in Japan and the US felt vindicated in their views that cloned animals have short lifespans when Dolly was put to sleep at six-and-a-half years old after suffering from a progressive lung disease. Despite this, Dolly gave birth to six healthy lambs during her short lifetime.

TIMELINE

1938 Cloning is first envisioned by German Dr Hans Spemann, who proposes a form of nuclear transfer in cells.

1973 Paul Berg and Stanley N. Cohen successfully splice a gene for the first time.

1993 The first human embryos are cloned in America. Cells taken from defective human embryos are grown *in vitro* and then destroyed at the 32-cell stage.

1994 American Dr Ned First clones calves from the cells of early embryos.

1995 Dr Ian Wilmut creates the world's first cloned sheep, Megan and Morag, from embryo cells at the Roslin Institute in Edinburgh, Scotland

| 1938 | 1953 | 1973 | 1978 | 1984 | 1993 | 1994 | 1995 | 1996 |

1953 The structure of DNA (deoxyribonucleic acid) is discovered by Francis C. Crick and James D. Watson.

1984 Danish Dr Steen Willadsen clones a lamb.

1996 Dr Ian Wilmut and his team clone Dolly, the world's first sheep created from adult cells.

1978 The first child is conceived by *in vitro* fertilization (IVF).

1952
FIRST FROG

In 1952, American scientists Robert Briggs and Thomas King successfully cloned the first frog. To create the frog, the scientists used the same nuclear transfer technique that would be employed 44 years later to clone Dolly the sheep. This meant transferring the nucleus – or genetic material – from an early tadpole embryo into a frog egg that had had the nucleus removed. The resulting cell then grew into a tadpole. The experiment was an important breakthrough, because it showed that 'nuclear transfer' was a viable cloning technique. It also indicated that early embryonic cells are better for cloning than cells at later stages. Briggs and King found that those tadpoles cloned from more advanced embryos tended to grow into frogs with abnormalities.

1975
RARE RABBIT

In 1975, British scientist J. Derek Bromhall used a tiny glass straw to transfer the nucleus from a rabbit embryo into a rabbit egg cell without a nucleus. This method of transfer was necessary because mammalian egg cells are much smaller than those of frogs, so are harder to manipulate. Bromhall considered the experiment a success when a rabbit embryo began to develop a few days later. However, Bromhall did not carry his work to its conclusion by implanting the embryo into a rabbit mother's womb.

Scientists watch a cloned rabbit.

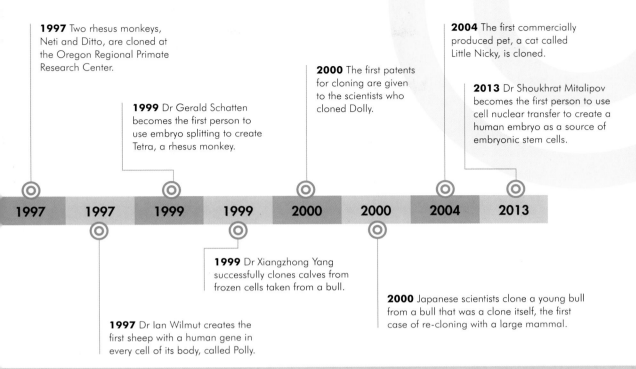

1997 Two rhesus monkeys, Neti and Ditto, are cloned at the Oregon Regional Primate Research Center.

1999 Dr Gerald Schatten becomes the first person to use embryo splitting to create Tetra, a rhesus monkey.

2000 The first patents for cloning are given to the scientists who cloned Dolly.

2004 The first commercially produced pet, a cat called Little Nicky, is cloned.

2013 Dr Shoukhrat Mitalipov becomes the first person to use cell nuclear transfer to create a human embryo as a source of embryonic stem cells.

1997	1997	1999	1999	2000	2000	2004	2013

1999 Dr Xiangzhong Yang successfully clones calves from frozen cells taken from a bull.

2000 Japanese scientists clone a young bull from a bull that was a clone itself, the first case of re-cloning with a large mammal.

1997 Dr Ian Wilmut creates the first sheep with a human gene in every cell of its body, called Polly.

1984
SPECIAL SHEEP

Danish scientist Steen Willadsen became the first person to successfully clone a mammal in 1984, when he used cells from early embryos to clone sheep. Willadsen did this by separating one cell from an eight-cell lamb embryo and fusing it into an egg cell without a nucleus. The resulting embryos were implanted into a surrogate mother sheep who went on to give birth to three lambs. Willadsen's experiment showed that a mammal could be cloned by nuclear transfer, even though the donor nuclei in this case came from early embryonic cells. Dr Ian Wilmut would take this one step further 13 years later by cloning a sheep from adult cells.

Dr Ian Wilmut.

1997
MONKEY MAGIC

In 1997, a team of US scientists led by Dr Gerald Schatten became the first to clone a primate, the closest animal relative to humans. Schatten's team used a different method to the one used to clone Dolly the sheep. Instead of transferring a nucleus into an empty egg cell, the scientists split the original cells in an embryo to make identical animals. The result was the cloning of two baby rhesus monkeys, a female called Neti and a male called Ditto. The cloning of the monkeys was seen as a groundbreaking moment. As monkeys have such similar DNA to humans, scientists hope that monkey clones can be used for the study of human ailments. They could also be harvested for stem cells, the master cells that can develop into any type of cell in the body.

1999
NATO BOMBS SERBIA

'Yugoslavia cannot exist without Kosovo! Yugoslavia will become disintegrated without Kosovo! Yugoslavia and Serbia will never give up Kosovo!'

– Former Serbian president Slobodan Milosevic expresses his views on a united Serbian state

The NATO decision to bomb Serbia came as a response to the atrocities committed by its military in the Kosovo War. But there was also a broader agenda. After nearly nine years of civil war in the former Yugoslavia, NATO wanted a line drawn underneath the peace deal it had brokered in Dayton in 1995. In 1999, it therefore called for 'the immediate termination of violence and repressive activities by the Milosevic government.' The trouble in Kosovo had begun in 1996, when the newly formed Kosovo Liberation Army (KLA) had started attacking Serbian politicians and police in its attempt to free the country from Serbian rule. To the KLA, Kosovo was occupied by an ethnic Albanian majority who sought independence. To Serbia, Kosovo was the one-time centre of the former Yugoslavia that was still inhabited by ethnic Serbians. In 1998, Serbian president Slobodan Milosevic decided to suppress the increasing attacks by the KLA and sent in his military to reassert Serbian control. Atrocities then committed by

the Serbian military forced a wave of refugees to flee from the area. After the similar horrors previously committed during the Yugoslav wars, NATO felt obliged to intervene. But after Milosevic reneged on a promise to withdraw his forces, the KLA regrouped and renewed their attacks. The Serbian military responded with a brutal counteroffensive that included a programme of ethnic cleansing against the Albanians. In response, the NATO airstrikes began against the Serbian military on 24 March 1999. The bombing lasted for 11 weeks and eventually included targets within the country's capital, Belgrade. By June, faced with the superior might of the NATO military and the dwindling support of his own people, Milosevic signed a peace accord. This agreed to the withdrawal of Serbian troops, the deployment of UN peacekeeping forces and the return of over 1.5 million displaced Albanians to Kosovo. In 2008, Kosovo finally won its independence from Serbia.

NATO releases a missile bound for Belgrade from one of its battleships stationed in the Adriatic Sea.

FLASHPOINT FACT

Among the atrocities committed by both Albanian and Serbian Kosovans during the Kosovo War, were claims of KLA organ theft from murdered Serbians.

TIMELINE

12th century
Kosovo lies at the heart of the Serbian empire under the Nemanjic dynasty.

1912 Serbia regains control of Kosovo from the Turks after the Balkan Wars.

1945 Kosovo is absorbed into the Yugoslav Federation.

1989 Yugoslav president Slobodan Milosevic strips Kosovo's rights of autonomy.

1990 Ethnic Albanian leaders declare independence from Serbia. Milosevic dissolves the Kosovo government.

1991 War breaks out in the Balkans.

| 1100s | 1389 | 1912 | 1918 | 1945 | 1974 | 1989 | 1990 | 1991 | 1992 |

1389 The Battle of Kosovo heralds 500 years of Turkish Ottoman rule.

1918 Kosovo becomes part of the kingdom of Serbia.

1974 The Yugoslav constitution recognizes the autonomous status of Kosovo.

1992 Albanian Ibrahim Rugova is elected president of the self-proclaimed republic of Kosovo.

1974
AUTONOMOUS KOSOVO

During the Balkan War of 1912, Serbia regained control of its medieval territory of Kosovo from the Turks and in 1918 Kosovo joined the kingdom of Serbia once more. Then, in 1945, Kosovo became part of the Federal People's Republic of Yugoslavia alongside the Balkan states of Serbia, Croatia, Bosnia-Herzegovina, Montenegro, Slovenia and Macedonia. However, Yugoslavia's communist leader Josip Broz Tito was willing to listen to Kosovo's claim for greater autonomy under its Albanian majority. In 1974, the Yugoslav constitution recognized the autonomous state of Kosovo, which gave the province a *de facto* self-government.

1987
KOSOVO SUPPRESSED

Serbians came to resent Kosovo's autonomy, especially those who made up the country's ethnic minority. As part of his rise to power, Slobodan Milosevic rallied a crowd of Kosovo Serbs who claimed they were being discriminated against by the Albanian community. In 1987, Milosevic was elected leader of Serbia's Communist party and in 1989, president of the country. Milosevic then proceeded to strip Kosovo of the autonomy given to the country in the 1974 constitution. In 1990, Albanian leaders declared Kosovo's independence from Serbia, and in response Milosevic sent in troops to dissolve the Kosovo government. Large numbers of Kosovo Albanians were fired from public positions and Albanian teachers were prevented from entering their schools.

Slobodan Milosevic addresses his Serbian people.

1995 The Dayton Agreement, brokered by US president Bill Clinton, officially ends the war in Bosnia.

April 1999 Hundreds of thousands of Kosovo Albanian refugees pour into neighbouring countries, reporting massacres and forced expulsions.

September 1998 NATO gives an ultimatum to Milosevic to stop his crackdown on Kosovo Albanians.

June 1999 President Milosevic agrees to withdraw troops from Kosovo and NATO calls off its air strikes. The UN sets up a Kosovo Peace Implementation Force (KFOR) and NATO peacekeepers arrive.

2008 Kosovo declares independence, which is recognized by the United States and Europe's major powers, but not Serbia.

1995	1998	1998	1999	1999	1999	2002	2008	2013

March–September 1998 Open conflict between the Serb police and the Kosovo Liberation Army (KLA) is followed by a brutal crackdown by the Serbian military.

March–April 1999 Internationally brokered peace talks between NATO and Serbia fail. NATO launches air strikes against Yugoslavia, lasting 78 days before Belgrade yields.

2002 Ibrahim Rugova is elected as president by the Kosovo parliament.

2013 The Kosovo government holds the first local elections supported by Serbia since the 2008 declaration of independence.

Bombed out buildings in Bosnia.

1991
YUGOSLAV WARS

In 1991, Slovenia, Croatia and Bosnia broke away from Yugoslavia and declared their independence. This led to the Serbian massacre of 1,700 Croats in the Croatian city of Vukovar in 1991 and the start of the Yugoslav wars. As the war raged, Kosovo began four years of non-violent resistance to Serbian rule under ethnic Albanian leader Ibrahim Rugova. In 1996, the Kosovo Liberation Army (KLA) was formed to make a more militant response to the oppressive Serbian rule. After the KLA stepped up its attacks on Serbian targets in 1997, the Serbian military issued a major offensive against the KLA stronghold in the Drenica region.

1999
AIR STRIKES

After reported atrocities that included murder, rape, torture and the mass expulsion of ethnic Albanians, NATO ordered air strikes against the Serbian government in 1999. On 24 April a bombing campaign by 1,000 NATO aircraft, supported by warship and submarine missiles, began against Serbian military targets. 'Duel-use' targets were also bombed, such as power stations and communications facilities. During an airstrike in Belgrade, NATO accidently fired on the Chinese embassy, killing three journalists and causing diplomatic tensions with China. Albanian citizens were also killed during an air strike after being used as a human shield by the Serbian military. After Milosevic was forced to withdraw his troops – because of air strikes crippling Serbia and also because of pressure from Serbia's one-time ally Russia – the NATO bombing ended on 10 June. Kosovo became supervised under the UN until an independence referendum was held three years later.

Y2K
THE MILLENNIUM BUG

'Pay attention to the things that are vulnerable in your life and make contingency plans…don't panic, but don't spend too much time sleeping, either.'

– Chairman of the US Senate's Special Committee on the Year 2000 Problem, Senator Robert Bennett, gives advice on how to prepare for Y2K

As the clocks struck midnight on the morning of 1 January 2000, nervous computer users around the world held their collective breath. While billions celebrated the end of the 20th century and the beginning of a new millennium, others waited for a computer catastrophe on a global scale. Many scenarios had been predicted as a result of the Year 2000 Problem or 'Y2K', also known as the Millennium Bug. Some prophesied that entire computer networks would crash on the stroke of midnight, causing nuclear power plant meltdowns, power grid failures and the deletion of bank and government databases. The problem was to do with the world's dependence on computer technology, which in the latter half of the 20th century became used for everything from telling us the time to storing information about our identities. However, in the 1980s it emerged that a fatal flaw had been accidently built into computer design – the date. To save memory, early computers had been programmed to use two digits to display the year. When the year was 1998 – or '98', as computers showed it – this caused no problem. But what would happen when the date clicked over from '99' to '00'? Many experts theorized that computers would think they had reverted back to the year 1900 and malfunction, crash or stop working altogether. In response, governments of the world ordered that all important computer networks, such as those running government departments, intelligence satellites, travel and transport, power grids and nuclear power plants, be upgraded. As the decade wore on, the world became gripped with upgrading its computers, spending between $300 and $600 billion worldwide, to make them 'Y2K compliant'. Then, on 31 January 1999, the big moment came – and then went, with barely a computer glitch in sight. So it was that the great event predicted to cap off the 20th century with a bang instead saw it out with a relieved sigh.

Concerned students at the end of last century ponder the possible effect of Y2K on their computer.

FLASHPOINT FACT

The next possible catastrophic computer glitch is forecast for the year 2038, when computers using 32-bit systems won't be able to cope with the change of date. This glitch has been dubbed 'Y2038'.

TIMELINE

1984 *Computers in Crisis* by Jerome and Marilyn Murray predicts worldwide computer system crashes at the turn of the millennium.

1993 Magazine *Computerworld* predicts Y2K compliance costs will reach $74 billion by 1999.

1998 A Washington computer firm warns in its 'Y2K Weather Report' that the Millennium Bug will be used as an excuse to put martial law into effect by unscrupulous governments.

October 1998 The US Year 2000 Information and Readiness Disclos[ure] Act encourages American compan[ies] to share Y2K information.

July 1999 US president Bill Clinton signs the Year 2000 Readiness and Responsibility Act, which limits the legal liability of companies that suf[fer] problems as a result of Y2K.

1984	1985	1993	1995	1998	1998	1998	1999	1999

1985 The Year 2000 Problem is introduced as a discussion forum on a Usenet site, by user Spencer Bolles.

1995 David Eddy, a Massachusetts programmer, coins the acronym 'Y2K'.

May 1998 US president Bill Clinton orders the government to work with businesses to make sure that the country's information systems are kept safe against the Y2K threat.

April 1999 The European Commission warns that many Europea[n] nations are not yet Y2K compliant.

FLASHPOINTS

1995
Y2K BUILD UP

The problems associated with Y2K were first thought to have been flagged up in a 1984 book called *Computers in Crisis* by Jerome and Marilyn Murray, which was then republished in 1996. The Y2K subject became an increasingly popular subject of speculation among online discussion groups from the mid- to late 1980s. The term Y2K itself was thought to have been coined by Massachusetts programmer David Eddy in 1995. As the subject of Y2K readiness picked up pace in the media, governments and businesses around the world began hiring technology teams to upgrade their computers and computer systems and make them 'Y2K compliant'.

1998
CLINTON ACTS

In May 1998, US president Bill Clinton ordered the government to work with businesses to make the nation's information networks secure. In October of that year, Clinton signed the Year 2000 Information and Readiness Disclosure Act, a law that encouraged US companies to share their Y2K information, products and practices. At the end of the year, a Y2K preparedness survey by Cap Gemini America, a New York computer consulting firm, showed that among 13 economic sectors in America, central government was the least prepared for Y2K.

President Clinton attempts to make the US Y2K compliant.

September 1999
A study of US companies reports that 44 per cent will not be Y2K compliant by the year 2000 deadline.

October 1999 Cap Gemini America predicts Y2K preparedness will cost the US $858 billion.

November 1999 The US Department of Commerce warns that costs to repair the damage caused by Y2K will reach $114 billion.

1 January 2000 No major Millennium Bug problems are reported. Japan said its radiation-monitoring equipment had failed at its Ishikawa nuclear plant, but that there was no risk to the public.

1999	1999	1999	1999	1999	1999	2000	2000

October 1999 London-based International Monitoring reports that Y2K could lead to $1.1 trillion in damages worldwide.

August 1999 A US survey shows that 43 per cent of the country's 150 large companies are restricting leave for December 1999 and January 2000.

December 1999
A poll by *USA Today* reported that only seven per cent of Americans said they expected major problems to result from Y2K, while 55 per cent said they thought the effects would last only a few days.

2 January 2000 John Koskinen says, 'One of the questions you've begun to see surface is, "Well, has this all been hype?" The answer is no…I think that we should not underestimate the nature of the problem that was originally there.'

1999
EUROPE UNPREPARED
In 1999, a report by the European Commission warned that efforts to prepare for Y2K were insufficient in many European Union member countries. The exception was Britain, whose government announced in 1999 that its armed forces and military computer systems would be Y2K compliant by the end of the year. The government said its military would then be available to provide support to local police, utility companies, transportation systems and emergency services if these failed because of the Millennium Bug.

2000
Y2K OVER
As the 21st century dawned and it became clear that the world's computer systems were still operational, the media was filled with stories of relieved governments and businesses. Relief, however, soon turned to anger as many started to believe that the issues surrounding Y2K had been greatly exaggerated. The finger was pointed at technology experts and computer engineers, who had often made small fortunes ensuring that computers and systems had been upgraded in time for the year 2000. The Y2K experts responded by saying that the Millennium Bug threat had been real and that the worldwide Y2K preparedness effort had ensured that it had been seen off, and a worldwide catastrophe averted.

Y2K merchandise.

Y2K was taken deadly seriously by the US military.

INDEX

PICTURE CREDITS

Alamy akg-images 24r; imagebroker 133b

Corbis Jacek Bednarczyk/epa 164; Matthew Polak/Sygma 165; Najlah Feanny/Saba 163; Ralph White 5l; Richard Ellis/Demotix 172; Srdjan Suki/epa 168; Vasily Fedosenko/Reuters 137a

Getty Images AFP: 114, Alain-Pierre Hovasse 157r, Alexander Joe 151, Alexander Nemenov128, Anatoly Sapronyenko 155, Dima Korotayev 129l, Georges Gobet 160, Gerard Malie 141, Johannes Eisele 159, John MacDougall 139, Manuel Ceneta 143, Mark Leffingwell 173l, Odd Andersen 153r, OFF 42r, Pierre Verdy 150, Romeo Gacad 171, Sergei Supinsky 136, S Joberg 127r, Toru Yamanaka 161, Vitaly Armand 156, Volodymyr Shuvayev 137b; Alex Bowie 127l; Andreas Rentz 149; Apic 121; Central Press 44; Chip HIRES/Gamma-Rapho 144, 145; Daily Express/Archive Photos 95l; Dean Purcell 78; Ed Giorandino/NY Daily News Archive 111b; Fine Art Images/Heritage Images 28r, 89; Gamma-Keystone 53, 61l, 72, 91, 93r, 98, 109; H William Tetlow/Fox Photos 97; Hulton Archive: 5r, 34, 51, 57, 58, 101, 104, R McPhedran/Daily Express 73b, Three Lions 107l; Imagno: 35l, 55b, Votava 107r; Imperial War Museum via Getty Images 31; Jay Florian Mitchell/Archive Photos 38l; Jeff Overs/BBC News & Current Affairs via Getty Images 153; Keystone 47, 73, 111a; Library of Congress/digital version Science Faction 7, 8; The Life Picture Collection: Art Rickerby 99r, Carl Mydans 74, Carlo Bavagnoli 119, Don Cravens 85l, 85r; George Silk 93, Hank Walker 103r, J R Eyerman 69l; Larry Burrows 113, 115, Loomis Dean 117, Ralph Morse 122, Time Life Pictures/Department Of Defense (DOD) 76, Time Life Pictures/Mansell 18, 20r, 32, Time Life Pictures/NASA 120, Urbano Delvalle 173r; Malcolm Linton/Liaison 132, 169; Mark and Colleen Hayward 94, 110; Max Scheler/K & K 95r; Phil Dent 133a; Pictorial Parade 79; Popperfoto 16, 42, 71, 81l; The Print Collector: 92, Ann Ronan 21, Oxford Science Archive 11, 13; Reg Lancaster 118; Roland Neveu/LightRocket via Getty Images 126; Science & Society Picture Library 9, 12, 38r, 39, 99l; Shone/Gamma-Rapho135; Stock Montage 10; Topical Press Agency 4, 24l, 30, 33r; 35r, 37; UIG: Photo12 15, 43, Photofusion 131, Sovfoto 27, 60, 61r, 87, 88, 125, 157l, TCI/Marka17a, Universal History Archive 23, 25, 28l, 41, 46r, 49, 50, 65, 67, 68, 69; ullstein bild: 17b, 19, 20l, 54, 55a, 59l, 62, 75, 77, 80, Astro-Graphs 123, Czechatz 140, joko 59r, Rühe 45, 46l, von der Becke 105, White Night Press/Irina Bernstein 129r; US Navy 167, Underwood Archives 33l, 83, 103l

Library of Congress 63

Press Association Images AP 147

Shutterstock Anton Rogozin 81r

Thinkstock Photos.com 64l